GIVE YOURSELVES A BREAK

How God Restores the Hearts of Men Who Carry Too Much

David Proctor

Scripture quotations are taken from the Holy Bible, New Living Translation (NLT), New International Version® (NIV®), King James Version (KJV), and the Amplified Bible (AMP), unless otherwise noted.

ISBN: 979-8-9962551-1-5 (Paperback)

Printed by GranVision Press., in the United States of America.

First printing edition 2026

GranVision Press
875 W. Poplar Avenue, Suite 23-293
Collierville, TN 38017

www.GranVisionPress.com

For every man who picked up this book—

Thank you. I wrote it with you in mind.

This isn't just a collection of words. It's a lifeline.

CONTENTS

Acknowledgements

First and foremost, I thank God—my Father, Jesus, my Savior, and the Holy Spirit, my advocate, and my Healer. Without His grace, none of this would exist. He met me in my lowest valleys, gave me strength when I was empty, and whispered purpose into my pain. Every page of this book is a testimony to His faithfulness.

To my incredible family: thank you for walking with me, loving me, and believing in me. To my beautiful wife, Shannon—your love restored so much of what was broken in me. You've stood by me, encouraged me, and reminded me of what true partnership looks like. You are a gift, and I am grateful every single day.

To my children—Valencia, Jared, Anthony, and to the memory of my daughter Brittany—you are my heart, my joy, and my motivation. Everything I write, everything I hope to become, is in part because of you. I pray this book encourages you to live boldly, love deeply, and walk closely with God.

To my brothers, C.W., Greg, and my brother in heaven, Manuel—you are strong, faithful men. We are who we are because of the example Daddy set before us. Thank you for walking this life with me, for being sounding boards, friends, and warriors in the faith. To my sisters, Nadean, Linda, and Lisa—my love runs deep, and you always provide a calm listening ear.

To my father, Wardell Proctor—Daddy, your life of integrity, hard work, and quiet strength is the foundation of the man I am today. You showed me what love looks like through action, and I honor you with every word written here. To my mother, Mary Proctor—there is not a day that goes by that I don't think of you and the unconditional love you showed our entire family. I miss you so much, Myme.

To every man who picked up this book—thank you. I wrote it with you in mind. This isn't just a collection of words. It's a lifeline. I pray it gives you permission to feel, to hope, and to heal.

To every mentor, pastor, friend, and brother who poured into me during my own healing journey—your words mattered. Your presence mattered. Thank you for standing in the gap when I couldn't stand on my own.

And finally, to every man who reads these pages and chooses to live with more grace, vulnerability, and courage—I honor you. The world needs more of who you are becoming.

Preface

This book began in the quiet places—between prayers, tears, and moments of deep reflection. I didn't write this to teach men how to be "tough" or how to hide better. I wrote it because I've been broken. I've been the man who smiled on the outside while bleeding on the inside. I've faced divorce, emotional loss, spiritual disconnection, and the ache of not having my daughter as a part of my daily life after that divorce. And I've found that healing isn't just possible—it's necessary.

What changed my life wasn't a formula. It was surrender. It was time alone. It was my personal relationship with Jesus. It was the grace and mercy of God that brought me through.

I didn't write this book because I had all the answers. I wrote from a place of humility, hidden shame, and a desire to examine what it means to heal from a past littered with mistakes. I wrote it because I wanted to help other men realize that they are more powerful than they think. I wanted to show that you can make it through the storms of life with patience, honesty, and the courage to face your faults. You may not agree with everything I say—and that's okay. My heart is in the right place, and I want only the best for you.

I wrote it because I've been there.

I've worn the mask.

I've held in tears.

I've smiled while breaking inside.

I've carried more than I could handle because I thought that's what a man was supposed to do.

This book is for the man who's been told to "man up" one too many times.

For the man who was never taught how to feel.

For the man who hid his true emotions and walked around doubting himself.

For the man who is leading, providing, protecting—but silently suffering.

For the man who wonders if he is enough.

Brother, you are more than enough.

This book is not written from perfection but from process. I am still growing, still learning, still healing. I have learned to give myself a break—to stop being so hard on myself, to be patient when I find myself on the wrong path.

I hope that by sharing my journey, you will feel less alone. I hope you will embrace patience and self-compassion. I hope you will move forward with courage.

I've had to unlearn the lies of toxic masculinity and rediscover what it means to be a man through the lens of God's Word. Real men have emotions, fears, and doubts.

But real men pray.

Real men fail, get up, and try again.

Real men love deeply, lead humbly, and live authentically.

Real men are not defined by the weight they carry—but by the One who carries them.

This book isn't about shaming men. It's about freeing them.

It's about giving you permission to stop performing and start healing.

To stop pretending and start growing.

To stop carrying burdens alone and start walking with God.

You may cry reading these pages. Let them flow, brother.

You may get angry. That's okay too.

But I pray you'll walk away changed—lighter, freer, stronger, and more connected to the man God created you to be.

Because the world doesn't need more hollow men.

It needs whole men.

Welcome to the journey.

Thank you for joining me.

CHAPTER 1

The Mask

I want to start by asking you something. Not the question you'd expect. Not "how are you doing" — because you already know the answer you'd give to that, and it probably isn't the truth.

I want to ask you this: When was the last time you were fully honest with someone about what was actually happening inside you?

Not the edited version. Not the "I've been a little stressed but I'm good" version. The real version. The one that includes what keeps you up at night, what you're afraid of, what you've been carrying so long it doesn't even feel heavy anymore because you've forgotten what it felt like not to carry it.

For most men, that question lands somewhere uncomfortable. Because the honest answer is — it's been a while. Maybe a long while. Maybe you're not even sure who you'd tell, or how you'd start, or whether you have the language for it anymore.

That is not weakness.

That is what the mask does to a man over time.

HOW IT STARTS

Nobody hands you the mask. Nobody sits you down and says, "Here is how to hide who you are." It happens gradually, invisibly, through a thousand small moments that teach you the same lesson until you stop needing to be taught it.

For me, it started at home.

I grew up in the Deep South, one of seven children in a three-bedroom house — seven kids, two parents, one bathroom, no central air or heat. Space was tight and privacy was rare. My father left early every morning for his day job and came back just long enough to leave again for the night shift, cleaning warehouse buildings until late. He never complained. He never explained. He just worked — quietly, consistently, without drama. That was the model of a man I was watching from the time I could watch anything.

My mother ran the house. She was loving, but she was firm. Discipline was real in our home. And I remember — clearly, even now — that when she corrected us, when the sting of it made your eyes well up, she would look at you and say:

"You better not cry."

Three words. And they went in deep.

Not because she was cruel. She wasn't. She was a woman raising seven children in difficult circumstances and she was teaching us the only way she knew how to survive: toughen up, keep moving, don't let pain slow you down. She learned it somewhere too. That's how it gets passed down — not maliciously, just automatically, the way we hand things to the next generation without realizing what we're handing them.

But that lesson lodged inside me like a splinter. It joined everything else the world was already saying. Don't cry. Man up. Shake it off. Handle it. And by the time I was old enough to start making decisions about who I was going to be, I had already made the most important one without realizing it.

I was going to be the man who didn't need anything.

WHAT WEARING IT FEELS LIKE

I remember wearing hand-me-down clothes as a boy and feeling the shame of it when other kids made jokes. I would smile. I would deflect. I would make it seem like it didn't bother me. And then later, alone, where no one could see, I would let myself feel it.

That pattern — perform on the outside, feel in private — became the architecture of my emotional life for years. And I got good at it. Extremely good. Good enough that the people closest to me often had no idea what was happening beneath the surface. Good enough that I sometimes had no idea what was happening beneath the surface.

That is the insidious thing about the mask. It starts as something you put on consciously, in moments when showing your true face feels unsafe. But over time it stops being something you wear and becomes something you are. Or at least something you think you are. The line between performing strength and believing you have no other choice gets thinner and thinner until it disappears entirely.

I wore that mask for years as an adult. Through seasons of struggle, I kept private. Through a marriage that was fracturing while I maintained the appearance of a man who had it handled. Through grief I did not know how to name, let alone share. Through moments of failure I absorbed silently because asking for help felt like it would cost me the only thing I still felt sure of — the image of a man who could handle his life.

What I did not understand then, and what I want to say to you directly now, is this:

The mask was not protecting me. It was isolating me.

Every time I put it on, I was choosing the appearance of strength over the possibility of genuine connection. And genuine connection — with my family, with God, with the men around me who were probably struggling with the same things — was exactly what I needed most and what the mask made impossible.

WHAT IT COSTS

The mask costs more than most men realize until the bill comes due.

It costs intimacy. You cannot be fully known while wearing it. And if you cannot be fully known, you cannot be fully loved — not in the way that actually reaches you, that actually heals something, that makes you feel less alone. You can be admired from behind the mask. You can be respected. But you cannot be loved all the way through it, because the people who love you cannot reach what you are hiding.

It costs your relationship with God. I know that might sound strange, but I lived it. I would pray, and my prayers were managed. Composed. Spiritually presentable. I was not bringing God the actual contents of my life — I was bringing Him the version I thought He wanted to see. And the closeness I was aching for never came, because closeness requires honesty, and I would not be honest about how broken I really was. I kept showing up to God polished and put-together, when what He wanted was just the real me. I was too busy appearing fine, even to Him.

And it costs you yourself. A man who wears a mask long enough stops knowing where the mask ends and he begins. He loses access to his own interior life. He stops being able to name what he feels. He becomes a stranger to his own heart. And then one day he wakes up in a life that looks successful from the outside and feels completely empty from the inside, and he does not know how it happened or what to do about it.

That is not living. That is performing.

WHEN THE MASK BEGINS TO CRACK

Here is what I know about the mask: it does not hold forever.

It cracks. Sometimes slowly — through accumulated exhaustion, through the quiet weight of years of pretending. Sometimes suddenly — through a loss, a failure, a moment that hits harder than anything the mask was built to handle. Either way, there comes a point where it can no longer hold what is behind it.

For me it was not one dramatic moment. It was a series of them. Moments where I felt something rising in me that I did not have a name for. Moments where the distance between who I was presenting and who I actually was became too wide to maintain. Moments where I was tired — not physically tired, but tired in the way that has no cure except honesty.

And in those moments, something in me finally stopped performing long enough to say to God: I cannot keep doing this.

That was the beginning.

Not of a perfect man. Not of a man who had it figured out. But of a man who was done hiding, at least from God. And that small act of honesty — bringing the actual, unedited version of myself to the one who already knew every word before I said it — started something in me that years of appearing strong had never been able to start.

God does not force the mask off. He does not shame you for wearing it. He waits. He is patient in a way that is almost impossible to understand until you experience it — patient the way only someone who has never stopped loving you can be patient. He waits for the moment you finally get tired enough of pretending to try something else.

And when that moment comes, He does not meet you with judgment.

He meets you with the kind of grace that says: You can take it off now. I've been here the whole time.

THIS IS WHERE YOUR JOURNEY STARTS

I wrote this book for the man who is tired.

Not tired from working hard — though you probably are that too. Tired from performing. Tired from managing the image. Tired from carrying things alone that were never meant to be carried alone. Tired from saying "I'm fine" so many times that you've almost convinced yourself.

You picked up this book for a reason. Something in you recognized the title. Something in you is ready — maybe not to take the mask all the way off, not yet, but at least to admit it is there. At least to sit for a moment with the question of what it has cost you and what might be possible without it.

That is enough to start.

You are not broken.

You were conditioned. And what was learned can be unlearned — not easily, not all at once, but genuinely, with time and honesty and the grace of a God who has been waiting for you to stop pretending you do not need Him.

This is the beginning of your journey.

Not toward perfection.

Toward freedom.

And it starts with one honest admission:

The mask is not who I am.

• • •

REFLECT

1. When did you first put the mask on — and what was happening in your life at that moment that made hiding feel necessary?
2. What is one thing you are carrying right now that nobody in your life knows about? What has keeping that private cost you?
3. If you could say one completely honest thing to God right now — no spiritual language, no performance — what would it be?

CHAPTER 2

The Cost of Silence

Silence has a way of shaping a man. Not the peaceful kind of silence — the kind that restores your soul or gives you space to breathe. I'm talking about the heavy silence. The silence that sits on your chest. The silence that grows inside you when you've been holding too much for too long. The silence that becomes a lifestyle because you were never taught how to speak your truth.

Most men don't choose silence.

We inherit it.

We learn early that our emotions make other people uncomfortable. We learn that our pain is inconvenient. We learn that our fears are embarrassing. And so, little by little, we stop sharing. We stop expressing ourselves. We stopped reaching out. We stop letting people in.

We become experts at silence.

But silence has a cost.

It costs us connection.

It costs us intimacy.

It costs us the ability to be known.

It costs us the freedom to be honest.

It costs us the chance to heal.

And for many men, silence becomes the place where we hide our deepest wounds.

LEARNING SILENCE EARLY

Growing up, I didn't talk about what bothered me. I didn't talk about the things that hurt me. I didn't talk about the moments that made me feel small or ashamed. I didn't talk about the pressure I felt to be strong, to be responsible, to be the one who held everything together.

I learned to keep it all inside.

I learned to smile when I was hurting.

I learned to laugh when I was overwhelmed.

I learned to stay quiet when I needed help the most.

And the world applauded me for it.

People said things like, "You're so strong," or "You never complain," or "You always handle everything so well." They meant it as a compliment, but they had no idea that my silence wasn't strength — it was survival. It was the only way I knew how to cope.

But silence doesn't stay silent forever.

It builds.

It grows.

It presses against the walls of your heart until something cracks.

WHAT MY SILENCE ACTUALLY COST ME

I want to be honest with you in a way I was not honest with the people who loved me for far too long. My silence was not noble. It was not protective. It was not a sign of strength. It was avoidance dressed up as endurance. And it cost me more than I knew how to measure at the time.

I was emotionally absent in relationships where I should have been fully present. I had a wife who needed a husband she could reach, and too many times she reached for me and found a wall instead of a man. I had children who needed a father who could sit with them in the hard moments, not just showing up for the good ones. And I had a God who was waiting for me to stop performing long enough to let Him in — and I kept Him at arm's length too, because I thought even He needed the strong version of me.

Looking back now, I grieve those seasons. I grieve the conversations I didn't have. I grieve the moments of connection I missed because I was too proud, too afraid, or too conditioned to believe that speaking up made me less of a man. I can't undo those years. I can't reclaim what silence swallowed. And that is a regret I carry with honesty and humility.

But here is what I also carry: gratitude. Because God, in His mercy, did not leave me in that silence. He used the very damage my silence caused to bring me to a breaking point — and in that breaking, He began to build something better. The losses I experienced, the relationships that strained, the loneliness I felt even in a room full of people — none of it was wasted. God used all of it to pry open a heart that had been shut for too long.

I am not the man I was. And that is entirely His grace.

For some men, the crack in the armor shows up as anger — quick, sharp, and often misunderstood by the people around them. For others, it shows up as withdrawal, a quiet retreat into themselves where they become harder to reach and even harder to read. For many, it takes the form of depression, anxiety, or a kind of emotional numbness that makes life feel muted and distant. And for countless men, the fracture reveals itself most clearly in the relationships closest to them.

Silence never stays contained inside a man. It spills into the lives of everyone connected to him. When a man doesn't speak, the people who love him are left guessing. They don't know what he's feeling, what he needs, how to support him, or how to reach him. Over time, they may even stop trying — not because they've stopped caring, but because they no longer know how to break through the walls he's built.

I've lived that reality. I've seen the quiet damage silence can do. I've watched relationships strain and suffer because I didn't know how to express what was happening inside me. I lost moments where I should have spoken up. I lost opportunities to be honest. I lost the chance to let people love me in the places I was hurting. Silence doesn't just keep the world out — it keeps healing out too.

THE LIES SILENCE TELLS

Silence convinces a man that no one will understand him.

Silence convinces him that his pain is his burden alone.

Silence convinces him that speaking up will make him look weak.

Silence convinces him that he must endure everything without complaint.

But silence lies.

It tells a man he's protecting others from his pain, when in reality, he's protecting himself from vulnerability. It tells him he's being strong, when in reality, he's avoiding the truth. It tells him he's holding everything together, when in reality, he's slowly falling apart.

I believed those lies for years. I genuinely thought I was sparing people by not burdening them. I thought I was being responsible. I thought silence was a form of love. But the people who loved me didn't need me to carry it alone — they needed me to let them in. My silence didn't protect them. It disconnected us. And by the time I understood that, some of the damage was already done.

I've learned that silence is often rooted in fear — fear of being misunderstood, fear of being judged, fear of being seen as less than the image we've worked so hard to keep. But fear is not from God. Scripture reminds us in 2 Timothy 1:7 (NLT), "*For God has not given us a spirit of fear and timidity, but of power, love, and self-discipline.*" Yet many men live in fear every day — fear of being honest, fear of being vulnerable, fear of being known.

And that fear keeps us silent.

Silence creates confusion.

Silence creates frustration.

Silence creates emotional distance.

Silence creates misunderstandings.

And eventually, silence creates resentment — on both sides.

I've seen relationships fall apart not because of betrayal or conflict, but because of silence. Because one person didn't know how to express what they were feeling, and the other person didn't know how to reach them. Silence becomes the loudest voice in the relationship.

Silence doesn't just affect how we relate to others — it affects how we relate to ourselves. When a man stays quiet long enough, he begins to lose touch with his own emotions. He stops recognizing what he feels. He stops trusting his instincts. He stops acknowledging his needs. He becomes a stranger to his own heart.

That's the hidden danger of silence: it disconnects a man from himself. When I was a young man, I struggled to find direction. There was a restless emptiness inside me I couldn't name. I wasn't angry, but I couldn't find peace. I wasn't sad, but joy seemed distant. I was functioning but not truly living. Even when surrounded by people, I felt alone and disconnected. It wasn't until I turned to church and began building a relationship with God that I finally discovered purpose, connection, and a sense of belonging.

That's what silence does.

It numbs you.

It dulls your emotional senses.

It makes you believe that feeling nothing is better than feeling too much.

But God didn't create us to be numb. He created us to feel. He created us to connect. He created us to speak truth. He created us to live in relationship — with Him and with others.

When a man silences his emotions, he silences the very part of himself that God wants to heal.

Silence doesn't just affect a man's emotions or his relationships — it eventually affects his relationship with God. Not because God stops speaking, but because we slowly stop listening. Silence has a way of convincing us that God doesn't want to hear our struggles, that our weaknesses somehow disqualify us, or that we need to pull ourselves together before we come to Him. But Scripture never supports that kind of silence. The Word urges us to lean on Jesus, to cast our cares on Him, to cry out to the God who neither slumbers nor sleeps.

The truth is that God invites us to come exactly as we are — broken, confused, overwhelmed, and honest. He invites us to bring our fears, our doubts, our failures, and our pain. He invites us to speak, not because He needs the information, but because we need the release. God knows that healing begins the moment we stop hiding and start talking.

Quiet endurance is not the same as healing. A man can carry his silence for years and still feel every ounce of its weight.

THE TURNING POINT

There comes a point when silence becomes too heavy to carry. A point when the weight of unspoken emotions begins to crush the parts of us we've tried so hard to protect. And for many men, that moment becomes a turning point.

For me, the turning point wasn't dramatic. It wasn't a breakdown or a crisis. It was a quiet realization — one that came slowly, almost gently. I realized that my silence was costing me more than my honesty ever could. I realized that the people who loved me weren't asking me to be perfect — they were asking me to be present. They were asking me to be real. They were asking me to let them in.

And I realized something even deeper:

God wasn't asking me to be silent. I had chosen silence out of fear.

Fear of being misunderstood.

Fear of being judged.

Fear of being seen as weak.

Fear of disappointing the people who looked up to me.

Fear of admitting that I didn't have everything under control.

But God never asked me to carry that fear. He never asked me to pretend. He never asked me to hide.

Psalm 62:8 says, "*Trust in Him at all times, you people; pour out your hearts before Him; God is our refuge.*" That verse changed me. It reminded me that God doesn't want the polished version of me — He wants the honest version. He wants the man behind the silence. He wants the heart behind the mask.

I am so grateful that He waited for me. I am grateful that His patience outlasted my pride. I am grateful that every door my silence closed, His grace eventually reopened. Not all of them the same way. Not all of them without consequence. But He redeemed what I was willing to bring to Him. And that is more than I deserved.

Brother, He wants the same from you.

Silence may feel safe, but it is not healing.

Silence may feel strong, but it is not strength.

Silence may feel familiar, but it is not freedom.

Healing begins the moment a man finds the courage to speak. Healing begins when he tells the truth — to himself, to God, and to the people who love him. Healing begins when he stops hiding behind silence and starts living in honesty.

This doesn't mean you have to share everything with everyone. It doesn't mean you have to open up to people who haven't earned your trust. But it does mean you must stop carrying everything alone. You must stop believing the lie that your silence protects you. You must stop convincing yourself that your emotions are a burden.

Your voice matters.

Your truth matters.

Your heart matters.

And the world needs the real you — not the silent version.

Whatever my silence cost me, God has been faithful to redeem. Not because I earned it, but because that is who He is. The mistakes were mine. The mercy was His. And the growth that came from facing both — that is the gift I am still unwrapping, one honest conversation at a time.

This chapter is an invitation to break the silence.

Not all at once.

Not in a dramatic moment.

But slowly, intentionally, courageously.

Because the cost of silence is too high.

And the freedom on the other side of honesty is too great to ignore.
You were not created to suffer in silence.
You were created to live in truth.
You were created to be known.
You were created to be healed.
And this journey — this book — is your first step toward that freedom.

• • •

REFLECT

1. What has your silence cost you in your most important relationships — be specific and honest with yourself.
2. Is there someone in your life right now who needs to hear something you have been holding back? What is stopping you?
3. If you could tell God one thing you have never spoken out loud, what would it be?

CHAPTER 3

Permission to Feel

Let me say something to you that nobody probably said to you growing up. You are allowed to feel things.

Not just the acceptable ones — pride when you win, determination when you push through, satisfaction when you provide. I mean the ones you were taught to bury. The sadness you swallowed. The fear you smiled through. The loneliness you carried into rooms full of people and never once mentioned. The grief that never got a funeral because somebody needed you to be strong.

You are allowed to feel all of it.

I know that sounds simple. Maybe even obvious. But for most men — and I mean men who are otherwise capable, faith-filled, hardworking, decent men — those words land like something foreign. Because we were not raised to feel. We were raised to function.

Think about it. From the time you were a boy, what did you get rewarded for? Pushing through. Staying steady. Not making it a big deal. Getting back up without making noise about the fall. The men around you modeled endurance, not emotion. And so, you became what you were shown — a man who could carry a lot without saying much.

And here is the part nobody talks about: that worked. For a while, it actually worked. You got things done. People depended on you. You held it together when others couldn't. You built a reputation for being solid, reliable, unshakeable. And part of you was proud of that, because you had earned it.

But somewhere along the way — and if you are honest, you probably know when — something started to go quiet inside you. Not peaceful quiet. Dead quiet. The kind of quiet that isn't rest, it's shutdown. The kind where you can sit at a dinner table with people who love you and feel absolutely nothing and not even be sure that something is wrong because this is just how you live now.

That's where I found myself.

WHAT SHUTDOWN ACTUALLY LOOKS LIKE

I didn't recognize it as shutdown at the time. I called it discipline. I called it maturity. I told myself that I had learned to manage my emotions, which sounded like growth. But what I had actually done was stop having them — or at least stop acknowledging them. And the difference between managing your emotions and suppressing them is the difference between a pressure valve and a sealed container.

Eventually, sealed containers fail.

For me it didn't come out in some dramatic breakdown. It came out in irritability. In distance. In being physically present with people I loved while being completely unreachable to them. My wife would ask how I was doing and I would say fine, not because I was lying exactly, but because I genuinely didn't know anymore. I had spent so long not checking that I didn't have access to the answer.

That is what emotional shutdown costs you. Not just the pain — you lose the joy too. You cannot selectively numb yourself to the difficult emotions without also going numb to the good ones. When you lock the door on grief, you lock it on gratitude too. When you close yourself off to fear, you close yourself off to wonder. It all goes quietly together.

I missed so much during those years. Not events — I showed up for events. I missed the interior experience of my own life. The texture of it. The depth of it. I was there, but I wasn't present. And you cannot get that time back.

THE LIE AT THE CENTER OF IT

Here is the lie men believe — and I believed it completely for a long time:

Feeling things is the opposite of being strong.

It isn't. It never was. That lie has just been passed down so many times, by so many well-meaning people, that it has become invisible. It lives in the phrase "man up." It lives in "shake it off." It lives in every moment a boy was told that his tears were embarrassing, that his fear was inconvenient, that his emotions were something to be managed rather than experienced.

And here is the damage that lie does: it doesn't just suppress your emotions. It makes you ashamed of them. So, when they surface — and they always surface eventually — they come with guilt attached. A man cries and immediately apologizes for it. A man admits he is scared and spends the next ten minutes walking it back. A man says "I'm not okay" and then immediately says "but I'll be fine" because he cannot tolerate being seen as weak for more than about four seconds.

That is not strength. That is shame doing what shame does — keeping you hidden.

Real strength is not the absence of emotion. Real strength is staying in the room with what you feel instead of running from it. It is looking at your own grief, your own fear, your own longing, and not flinching. That takes more courage than most of what men call being tough.

WHAT EMOTIONS ACTUALLY ARE

Your emotions are not your enemies. They are not weaknesses. They are not signs that something is wrong with you.

They are information.

Anger is telling you something crossed a line. Sadness is telling you something that mattered. Fear is telling you something feels unsafe. Grief is telling you something was worth loving. Joy is telling you something is aligned with who you actually are.

When you shut that system down, you don't become stronger. You become blind. You stop being able to read yourself. You stop being able to read the people around you. You stop being able to hear what God might be saying to you through the interior of your own experience.

I had to learn — slowly, and at some cost — that God was not intimidated by any of what I felt. Not the anger I carried at myself for years. Not the grief about Brittany that I had walked around rather than through. Not the fear that I had failed people who deserved better. Not the loneliness I felt even surrounded by people who loved me.

He was not surprised by any of it. He was not disappointed. He was not waiting for me to clean it up before He got close. He was already close. I was the one who was far.

The moment I stopped performing wellness I didn't have and started bringing God the actual contents of my heart — the mess of it, the weight of it — something shifted that years of trying to be spiritually adequate had never produced.

That is what honesty with God feels like. And it starts with being honest enough with yourself to admit what you actually feel.

THIS IS YOUR PERMISSION

I am not asking you to become someone who cries at commercials and processes everything out loud. I am not asking you to turn your internal life into a public event. That is not what this is.

I am asking you to stop lying to yourself.

Start there. In private. Just you and the truth of what is actually happening inside you. No audience. No performance. Just an honest look at what you are carrying and what it is costing you.

Because here is what I know: the man who cannot feel cannot fully love. He cannot be fully present. He cannot be fully known. And he cannot be fully healed, because you cannot heal what you refuse to acknowledge.

You were not built for half a life.

You were built to feel deeply, love honestly, and live in the full range of what it means to be human. God did not design the interior of a man to be a storage facility for everything he could not deal with. He designed it to be alive.

You have permission to feel.

Not because someone gave it to you.

Because it was always yours.

• • •

REFLECT

1. What emotion have you been carrying the longest without naming it? Say it out loud right now, even if you are alone.
2. When was the last time you felt something deeply and let yourself stay with it instead of moving past it? What happened?
3. What would change in your closest relationship if you were honest about what you actually feel, starting this week?

CHAPTER 4

The Father Factor

Every man carries the imprint of his father—whether that father was present, absent, loving, distant, encouraging, harsh, or somewhere in between. A father shapes a boy's understanding of strength, identity, responsibility, and even God. Sometimes that influence is obvious, and sometimes it hides quietly beneath the surface, shaping our decisions, our relationships, and our sense of self without us even realizing it. The truth is, every man is, in some way, living out or reacting to the example of his father.

My father, Wardell Proctor, was a man of quiet strength. He wasn't loud, he wasn't flashy, and he didn't need to announce who he was. His presence spoke for him. He worked hard—harder than I understood at the time. He would leave early in the morning for his day job, come home for a short while, and then head back out to clean warehouse buildings at night. He didn't complain. He didn't boast. He simply did what needed to be done. As a child, I didn't fully appreciate the weight he carried. As a man, I look back and see the sacrifices he made with a deeper sense of gratitude.

Growing up in a house with seven children, space was limited and resources were stretched thin. But Daddy never let us feel poor. He never let us feel like we were lacking. He gave us stability, structure, and a sense of safety. He wasn't the type to sit down and have long emotional conversations, but his actions spoke volumes. He showed love through provision. He showed commitment through consistency. He showed strength through humility. And even though he didn't say much, his presence taught me more about manhood than any speech ever could.

Still, like many men, I didn't realize how deeply my father shaped me until I became an adult. I didn't realize how much of my identity was tied to his example. I didn't realize how many of my strengths—and my struggles—were connected to the lessons I learned from him. Fathers have a way of influencing us long after we've grown up. Their voices echo in our decisions. Their habits show up in our behavior. Their wounds sometimes become our wounds. Their strengths often become our strengths.

For some men, the father factor is a source of pride and gratitude. For others, it is a source of pain and confusion. Some men grew up with fathers who were present but emotionally distant. Others grew up with fathers who were physically absent but emotionally overwhelming. Some grew up with fathers who were loving but inconsistent. Others grew up with fathers who were harsh, unpredictable, or broken themselves. And some men grew up without a father at all, left to piece together their understanding of manhood from whatever examples they could find.

Regardless of the story, every man carries something from his father—whether it is a blessing to build on or a burden to overcome.

As I grew older, I began to see that my father's quiet strength shaped the way I approached life. I learned to work hard because he worked hard. I learned to endure because he endured. I learned to stay steady because he stayed steady. But I also learned to suppress my emotions because he rarely expressed his. I learned to keep things inside because that's what I saw him do. I learned to carry burdens silently because that's what he modeled. And while some of those lessons helped me survive, others kept me from healing.

That's the complexity of the father factor: it gives us both gifts and gaps.

And until a man is willing to examine both, he will continue to repeat patterns he doesn't understand.

As I grew into adulthood, I began to understand that my father's influence was woven into the fabric of who I was becoming. Some of the lessons he taught me were intentional lessons about hard work, respect, and responsibility. Others were unspoken, absorbed through observation, shaped by the rhythm of his life and the quiet strength he carried. I didn't realize it then, but I was learning what it meant to be a man simply by watching him move through the world.

Daddy wasn't a man of many words, but when he spoke, you listened. His voice carried weight, not because he demanded authority, but because he lived it. He didn't have to tell us to work hard—we saw it. He didn't have to tell us to be dependable, we watched him show up day after day, even when he was tired. He didn't have to tell us to be humble, we saw how he treated people with kindness and respect, no matter who they were. His life was a quiet sermon, preached not from a pulpit but from the example of consistency.

But like many fathers of his generation, emotional expression wasn't something he modeled. He loved us, but he didn't always say it. He cared deeply, but he didn't always show it in ways that were easy to interpret. He carried his burdens silently, believing that protecting his family meant shielding them from his struggles. And while that kind of strength is admirable, it also taught me—and many men like me—to internalize our emotions, to keep our pain to ourselves, and to equate vulnerability with weakness.

It took me years to understand that my father's silence wasn't a lack of love, it was the only language he knew. He came from a generation of men who were taught to survive, not to feel. Men who were taught to endure, not to express. Men who were taught to provide, not to process. Men who were taught that their value was measured by how much they could carry, not by how deeply they could connect.

And yet, even with those limitations, my father gave me something priceless: a foundation. He gave me a sense of identity. He gave me a model of integrity. He gave me a blueprint for perseverance. He gave me a picture of what it means to stand firm when life gets hard. Those gifts shaped me in ways I didn't fully appreciate until I became a man navigating my own storms.

GIFTS AND GAPS

But the father factor is not just about what we receive, it's also about what we lack. Every father, no matter how good, leaves gaps. Some gaps are small, others are deep. Some are easy to fill; others take years to understand. And many men spend their adult lives trying to reconcile the tension between the father they had and the father they needed.

For some men, that tension becomes a source of resentment. For others, it becomes a source of motivation. For many, it becomes a quiet ache—a longing for something they can't quite name. And for some, it becomes a cycle they unknowingly repeat with their own children.

I had to learn that honoring my father didn't mean ignoring the areas where I needed more. It didn't mean pretending he was perfect. It didn't mean denying the emotional gaps that shaped me. Honoring him meant acknowledging the fullness of his humanity, his strengths, his sacrifices, his limitations, and his wounds. It meant recognizing that he did the best he could with what he had, and that some of the things he couldn't give me were things he never received himself.

That realization softened me. It helped me see him not just as my father, but as a man—a man with his own story, his own struggles, his own fears, and his own unspoken dreams. And in seeing him more clearly, I began to see myself more clearly too.

Because every man's journey is, in some way, connected to the man who raised him—or the man who didn't.

As I continued to reflect on my father's influence, I realized that every man eventually reaches a point where he must evaluate the blueprint he inherited. Some parts of that blueprint are strong and worth keeping—values like integrity, work ethic, resilience, and responsibility. Other parts need to be examined, questioned, and sometimes replaced. This is not dishonoring our fathers; it is to acknowledge that they were human. They had strengths and weaknesses, victories and regrets, wisdom, and blind spots. And whether we realize it or not, we carry all of it with us into adulthood.

For many men, the father factor becomes most visible when they start families of their own. Suddenly, the lessons learned in childhood—both the spoken and unspoken ones—begin to surface. A man may find himself responding to his children the way his father responded to him, even if he promised himself, he would do things differently. Or he may find himself struggling to express affection because he never saw it modeled. Or he may feel pressure to be the "rock" of the family, even when he is emotionally exhausted. These patterns don't appear out of nowhere; they are the echoes of our upbringing.

I experienced this myself. There were moments when I realized I was repeating behaviors I didn't fully understand. I was carrying expectations that were never clearly defined. I was holding myself to standards that no one had spoken aloud. Much of it came from watching my father—his strength, his silence, his sacrifices. I admired him deeply, but I also had to acknowledge that some of the emotional habits I developed were a direct result of the things he didn't express. That realization didn't make me love him any less; it made me understand him more.

One of the most powerful shifts in my journey came when I began to see my father not just as "Daddy," but as a man. A man who had dreams of his own. A man who had fears he never voiced. A man who carried responsibilities that weighed heavily on him. A man who grew up in a world that didn't give him the space to explore his emotions. A man who did the best he could with the tools he had. When I saw him through that lens, compassion replaced confusion. Understanding replaced frustration. Grace replaced expectations.

This shift also helped me understand something important about myself: the emotional gaps I carried were not signs of failure—they were invitations.

Invitations to grow. Invitations to heal. Invitations to become more emotionally present than the generation before me. Invitations to break cycles that had been passed down unknowingly. Invitations to build a new blueprint for the men who would come after me.

GOD AS FATHER

This is where God's role becomes essential. Earthly fathers, no matter how good, are limited. They can guide us, but they cannot complete us. They can teach us, but they cannot heal us. They can love us, but they cannot fill every gap. Only God can do that. Scripture describes Him as a Father to the fatherless, a healer of the brokenhearted, and a restorer of what was lost. When we bring our father wounds to Him—whether those wounds come from absence, silence, harshness, or simply human imperfection—He meets us with compassion, not condemnation.

Understanding the father factor is not about assigning blame; it is about gaining clarity. It is about recognizing the forces that shaped us so we can take ownership of the men we are becoming. It is about acknowledging the influence of our past without allowing it to dictate our future. It is about honoring our fathers while also embracing the freedom to grow beyond their limitations.

And for many men, this becomes the turning point—the moment when they stop living as sons shaped by their past and start living as men shaped by purpose. As I continued to grow and reflect, I realized that understanding the father factor is not just about looking back, it is also about looking forward. Every man eventually reaches a point where he must decide what kind of father, mentor, or example he will be to the people who look up to him. Whether you have children or not, someone is watching you. Someone is learning from you. Someone is being shaped by your presence, your choices, your words, and your silence. And the question becomes: what will your influence produce?

For many men, this realization brings both hope and fear. Hope, because we want to give the next generation something better than what we received. Fear, because we are painfully aware of our own shortcomings. We worry that we will repeat the mistakes of our fathers. We worry that we will pass down the same emotional gaps. We worry that we will fail the people who depend on us. But the truth is, acknowledging those fears is the first step toward breaking generational patterns. You cannot change what you refuse to confront, and you cannot heal what you pretend does not exist.

One of the most freeing revelations in my journey was understanding that I am not bound to repeat the emotional patterns I inherited. I can honor my father's strengths without inheriting his silence. I can appreciate his sacrifices without adopting his emotional limitations. I can carry forward his integrity without carrying forward his inability to express vulnerability. And the same is true for every man. We are shaped by our fathers, but we are not defined by them. We can choose what we keep, what we release, and what we rebuild.

When I began to see God not just as Lord, but as Father, something shifted in me. I realized that I didn't have to earn His approval. I didn't have to hide my emotions. I didn't have to pretend to be strong. I didn't have to carry everything alone. I could bring Him my fears, my disappointments, my confusion, my longing, and my wounds. And instead of turning away, He met me with understanding. He met me with patience. He met me with healing. He met me with the kind of love that restores what life has broken.

This understanding helped me see my father with new eyes. It helped me appreciate his humanity. It helped me forgive the places where he fell short. It helped me honor the places where he excelled. And it helped me step into my own identity as a man—not as a reaction to my father, but as a reflection of God's shaping hand on my life. That shift brought peace. It brought clarity. It brought freedom.

Every man must eventually make peace with his father story. For some, that peace comes through gratitude. For others, it comes through forgiveness. For many, it comes through understanding. And for all of us, it comes through God's healing presence. The father factor is powerful, but it is not final. Your story does not end with what you inherited. It continues with what you choose to build.

This chapter is a chance to examine your father's story with honesty and grace. It's a moment to honor what was good, acknowledge what was painful, and place the broken pieces in God's hands. It's an opportunity to step into a new kind of manhood—one shaped not just by where you came from, but by purpose, healing, and God's steady guidance. And even as you face the parts of your story that feel unfinished or uncertain, you can hold on to this truth: "*He who began a good work in you will continue to perfect and complete it*" (Philippians 1:6, AMP). You are not destined to repeat the patterns you grew up with. You are not limited by the emotional gaps you inherited. You are not defined by the wounds you carry. You are a man in process, and God is faithfully shaping you from the inside out.

You are a man in process.

You are a man being shaped.

You are a man being healed.

You are a man becoming.

And as you continue this journey, you will discover that the greatest legacy you can leave is not perfection—it is transformation.

• • •

REFLECT

1. What did your father teach you about manhood—both through his words and his silence?
2. What is one gift your father gave you, and one gap he left?
3. How has your relationship with your earthly father shaped your view of God?

CHAPTER 5

When Strength Becomes a Burden

Every man reaches a point in his life when the very thing he thought made him strong begins to feel like a weight he can no longer carry. For years, we take pride in being dependable, steady, and unshakable. We become the ones people call when something goes wrong, the ones who hold the family together, the ones who keep calm in the storm. And for a while, that role feels honorable. It feels like purpose. It feels like identity. But over time, the pressure to always be strong can turn into a burden that slowly drains the life out of a man.

Most men don't realize when this shift happens. It's subtle. It begins with small things — moments when you feel tired but push through anyway, moments when you feel overwhelmed but keep going, moments when you feel afraid but refuse to admit it. You tell yourself that this is what men do. You tell yourself that you don't have the luxury of breaking down. You tell yourself that other people depend on you, so you must keep moving. And before long, strength becomes less of a gift and more of an expectation you can't escape.

I remember those seasons clearly — and I remember them with a regret I no longer try to minimize. I carried weight I should have shared. I stayed silent when I should have spoken. I kept going when I should have stopped and asked for help. I was so committed to appearing strong that I became inaccessible to the very people who loved me. And the cost of that — to my relationships, to my family, to my own soul — was real. I can name it now with honesty. I could not name it then because I was too deep inside the performance to see what it was doing to me.

THE HIDDEN WEIGHT

Many men live this way — functioning, providing, showing up, but slowly breaking down on the inside. We become experts at hiding our fatigue. We smile when we're tired. We nod when we're confused. We say "I'm good" when we're anything but. And the world rarely asks more because we've trained everyone, including ourselves, to believe that we are always okay.

But strength without rest is not strength — it is strain. And strain, when ignored, becomes suffering.

There is a difference between being strong and being hardened. Strength allows you to bend without breaking. Hardness makes you brittle. Strength allows you to endure with wisdom. Hardness forces you to endure without reflection. Strength allows you to ask for help when needed. Hardness convinces you that asking for help is failure. Many men confuse the two, and as a result, they carry burdens that were never meant to be carried alone.

The truth is, God never designed men to be self-sufficient. He designed us to be connected — to Him, to others, and to our own emotional lives. We were always meant to carry one another, to share the weight that grows too heavy for one set of shoulders. God knows we will face burdens too heavy to carry alone, and He built us to lean on each other when we do. Yet many men live without understanding that truth. We try to be our own strength, our own support, and our own source of endurance. Eventually, that self-reliance becomes a quiet form of bondage.

When strength becomes a burden, a man begins to lose himself. He becomes so focused on holding everything together that he forgets how to breathe. He becomes so committed to being dependable that he forgets how to be vulnerable. He becomes so accustomed to carrying weight that he forgets what it feels like to be free.

WHERE I FINALLY BROKE

I don't think I fully understood the weight I was carrying until it had already done significant damage. That is one of the harder truths I have had to sit with. By the time I recognized how much I was carrying, some of the consequences were already real. Relationships had been strained. Distance had grown where closeness should have been. And I had gone so long running on empty that I had lost touch with my own heart.

There was a season in my life when I was performing every role expected of me — husband, father, provider, minister — while silently falling apart on the inside. I was waking up exhausted. I was going to bed with the same weight I'd carried all day. I was smiling in rooms where I should have been honest. I was giving counsel I was not applying to my own life. I was encouraging other men to be vulnerable while I guarded my own heart like it was something to be ashamed of.

I told myself I was being responsible. I told myself that showing weakness would shake the people who depended on me. I told myself that a man in my position didn't have the luxury of falling apart. And every one of those things I told myself was a lie — a lie I believed so completely that I passed it off as conviction.

What I regret most is not the weight I carried. It's that I chose to carry it alone when God had already offered to carry it with me, and the people who loved me had already offered their hands. I said no to both — not out of strength, but out of pride. And that pride cost me peace I could have had years earlier. It cost people close to me a version of me that was present, open, and real. I grieve that. I don't say it to stay in the grief — I say it because naming it honestly is part of how I honor the growth that came after it.

Because growth did come. And that is where the gratitude lives.

Many men live in this quiet state of internal pressure. They wake up each morning already feeling behind. They carry the emotional weight of their families, their finances, their careers, and their private fears — all while pretending that everything is fine. And because they rarely express what they feel, the people around them assume they are strong enough to handle it all.

But strength without vulnerability becomes a trap. It convinces a man that he must always be the anchor, even when he is sinking. It convinces him that he must always be the provider, even when he is emotionally bankrupt. It convinces him that he must always be the protector, even when he is the one who needs protection.

One of the most dangerous consequences of carrying too much for too long is emotional numbness. When a man is overwhelmed, he doesn't always break down — sometimes he shuts down. He stops feeling deeply. He stops engaging fully. He stops noticing the small joys that once brought him life. He becomes present in body but distant in spirit. And because he is still functioning, still working, still providing, no one realizes that something inside him is slowly fading.

I know what it feels like to be surrounded by people yet feel alone. I know what it feels like to be admired for your strength while quietly drowning under the weight of expectations. I know what it feels like to be the one everyone depends on while having no idea where to place your own burdens. And I know what it feels like to reach a point where you realize that the strength you've been praised for is the very thing that is wearing you down.

REDEFINING STRENGTH

Here is the truth that changed me: God never asked me to carry everything. He never asked me to be the savior of my family. He never asked me to be the solution to every problem. He never asked me to be the one who holds everything together. That role belongs to Him alone. When I finally understood that, something inside me began to shift. I realized that my strength was never meant to replace God's presence — it was meant to reflect it.

Real strength is not about carrying more. It is about knowing when to let go. It is about recognizing your limits. It is about admitting your humanity. It is about trusting that God can handle what you cannot. And it is about allowing the people who love you to support you instead of shutting them out.

The turning point for me came when I realized that God was not asking me to be the strongest person in the room. He was asking me to trust Him. He was asking me to release the burdens I had been carrying alone. He was asking me to stop pretending that I had everything under control — not as a sign of failure, but as an invitation to experience His strength in a deeper way.

Matthew 11:28 says, "*Come to Me, all you who are weary and burdened, and I will give you rest.*" That verse is not a suggestion. It is a lifeline. It is God's way of saying, "You don't have to do this by yourself."

For a long time, I believed that letting go of burdens meant I was failing. I believed that asking for help meant I was weak. I believed that slowing down meant I was irresponsible. These beliefs were not rooted in truth — they were rooted in fear. Fear of disappointing others. Fear of losing control. Fear of being seen as less than the image I had worked so hard to maintain. But fear is a poor teacher, and it will always push a man toward isolation rather than connection, exhaustion rather than renewal, and self-reliance rather than surrender.

What I discovered when I finally let go — and I say this with genuine gratitude, not performance — is that God was not waiting to be impressed. He was waiting to be trusted. The moment I stopped trying to hold everything together and simply said, "Lord, I cannot do this," He met me in a way that years of striving never had. Not with condemnation. Not with disappointment. With rest. With relief. With the quiet steadiness of a Father who had been there all along, waiting for me to finally stop pretending I didn't need Him.

And I am grateful. Deeply, genuinely grateful. Not because the journey was easy — it was not. Not because I didn't make mistakes that had consequences — I did, but some of them were significant. But because God, in His mercy, did not waste a single one of those mistakes. He used the breaking to build something in me that the striving never could have produced. He used the exhaustion to teach me what rest actually feels like. He used the isolation to show me how much I needed connection. He used the weight to reveal what I had been carrying that was never mine to carry.

That is not something I take lightly. That is grace. And I am a different man because of it.

As I began to let go, I discovered something unexpected: the world didn't fall apart. The people who loved me didn't lose respect for me. My responsibilities didn't disappear, but they became lighter because I was no longer carrying them alone. Vulnerability doesn't diminish a man's strength — it deepens it. It allows him to connect more authentically, love more fully, and live more freely.

Letting go of the burden of strength also opened the door to healthier relationships. When I allowed myself to be honest about my struggles, the people around me felt safer being honest about theirs. When I admitted that I needed support, others felt permission to seek support too. When I stopped pretending to be invincible, the people closest to me finally felt like they could reach me.

Strength had built walls. Vulnerability built bridges.

One of the most transformative truths I learned is that God is not impressed by my ability to endure silently. He is moved by my willingness to surrender. He is not honored by my emotional numbness — He is honored by my honesty. And in that weakness, in that surrender, I found a peace that years of striving had never given me.

This chapter is not about abandoning strength. It is about redefining it. True strength is not the ability to carry everything — it is the wisdom to know what to carry, what to release, and who to trust with the weight. It is the courage to admit when you are overwhelmed. It is the humility to ask for help. It is the faith to believe that God can handle what you cannot. And it is the maturity to recognize that your worth is not measured by how much you endure, but by who you are becoming.

Whatever it cost me to learn that — and it cost something real — I would not trade the man I am becoming for the man I was trying so hard to be.

You do not have to be the strongest man in the room.

You do not have to carry everything alone.

You do not have to pretend you are unbreakable.

You do not have to hide your exhaustion.

You are allowed to rest.

You are allowed to ask for help.

You are allowed to be human.

And in that humanity, you will find a strength that is deeper, truer, and more sustainable than anything you have ever known.

• • •

REFLECT

1. When did your strength stop feeling like a gift and start feeling like a burden? Can you name the moment or the season?
2. What has carrying everything alone cost you — in your relationships, your health, your peace with God?
3. What would you lay down today if you truly believed the world wouldn't fall apart without you holding it up?

CHAPTER 6

The Weight of Expectations

Here is something I want you to sit with for a moment before we go any further. Think about what a real man looks like in your mind. Not what you would say if someone asked you — what you actually picture. The image that lives beneath the words.

I will tell you what mine looked like for most of my life. He never asked for help. He always had an answer. He did not complain. He provided without being asked. He led without showing doubt. He was steady when everyone else was falling apart. He had his finances in order, his family in line, his faith in good standing, and he handled whatever came at him without letting it show.

That man was exhausting to try to be.

And the thing is — nobody sat me down and handed me that image. I absorbed it. Piece by piece, over years, from the culture around me, from what I watched men get respected for, from what I watched men get dismissed for, from the silence of my father when things were hard and the pride I felt watching him carry it without breaking. I built an internal scoreboard without knowing I was building one. And then I spent decades trying to score on it.

I want to talk to you about what that actually cost. Not in theory. In real life.

WHAT LIVING UNDER A SCOREBOARD DOES TO A MAN

When you are living by an internal scoreboard — measuring yourself against an image of what a real man looks like — you are always either winning or losing. There is no rest in it. There is no just existing. Every day is an evaluation.

Did you provide enough? Handle enough? Hold it together enough? Did you look capable? Did anyone see the doubt? Did you slip? Did you recover fast enough that nobody noticed?

I lived that way for years. And the thing about a scoreboard is that it will let you feel good for a moment when things go well, but the moment something goes wrong, it is merciless. A financial hit. A relationship strain. A failure at work. A season where you just cannot seem to get it right. The scoreboard does not care about context. It does not care about what you were carrying. It just marks you down.

And when a man has been marked down enough times, one of two things happens. He either doubles down — pushes harder, carries more, performs bigger, because he cannot tolerate what failure says about him. Or he quietly gives up in some area of his life. Withdraws. Goes through the motions. Stops believing he is capable of getting it right, so he stops fully trying.

I have done both. I pushed when I should have rested, and I withdrew when I should have stayed.

Neither one was strength. Both were just different ways of responding to a pressure I had never questioned.

THE EXPECTATIONS NOBODY HANDED YOU

Here is the difficult part: most of the expectations crushing you were never actually placed on you by anyone.

Your wife did not tell you that you must never struggle financially or she will stop respecting you. You told yourself that.

Your children did not tell you that you must have all the answers or you will lose their confidence. You told yourself that.

God did not tell you that you must hold everything together or He will be disappointed. You told yourself that.

These expectations feel external because they are so deeply ingrained. But they are internal. You built them — often out of fear, often out of watching what happened to men who failed, often out of a genuine desire to be good at the things that matter. The motivation behind them is not always bad. The problem is what they demand of you in practice.

They demand that you never be human.

And you are human. Fully, unavoidably, beautifully human. You are going to have seasons where you cannot provide the way you want to. Seasons where you do not have the answers. Seasons where you are leading while you are lost, giving while you are empty, showing up while you are breaking. That is not failure. That is life. And the expectations that do not leave room for life will eventually break the man trying to live up to them.

I learned this the hard way.

There was a period of my life when I was trying to perform on every front simultaneously — as a man of faith, as a father, as a provider, as a leader — and I was doing it on empty. I was not replenishing anything. I was just spending, and spending, and spending, and telling myself that as long as I kept going it would somehow work out. But you cannot spend what you do not have indefinitely. Eventually, the account is empty and the withdrawals keep coming.

When that happened to me, I did not handle it gracefully. I did not sit down with the people who loved me and say, "I am running on empty and I need help." I white-knuckled it. I held on tighter. I doubled down on appearing capable. And that made everything harder and took longer than it needed to.

What I regret most is not that I struggled. Every man struggles. What I regret is that I wasted so much energy on the performance of not struggling rather than on actually getting the help that would have made the struggling shorter.

FREEDOM LOOKS LIKE PUTTING DOWN THE SCOREBOARD

The moment things started to change for me was not a dramatic moment of revelation. It was a quiet, private decision to stop measuring myself against an image that God never gave me.

That image — the man who never needs anything, never shows doubt, never admits difficulty — is not in Scripture. Show me that man in the Bible. Moses was terrified and tried to get out of his calling. David was a mess of emotion. Peter failed publicly and repeatedly. Paul wrote about his weakness so often that we sometimes miss how radical it was for a man of his stature to put it on paper.

The expectation of invulnerability is cultural. It is not biblical. And when you start to separate the two — when you start asking yourself "Is this expectation actually from God, or did I build it out of fear?" — you begin to find places to put things down.

Putting down expectations does not mean putting down responsibility. I want to be clear about that. It does not mean you stop providing, stop leading, stop showing up for the people who depend on you. Those things are real. Those things matter. But there is a difference between faithful responsibility and performance-based pressure. One comes from love and purpose. The other comes from fear and an image you are trying to protect.

When I finally started bringing my actual self to God — not the managed version, not the spiritually composed version, but the tired, uncertain, sometimes-failing man I actually was — something happened that years of performance had never produced. He met me there. Not with disappointment. Not with correction. With presence. With the quiet, steady companionship of a Father who had seen everything I was hiding and loved me anyway.

That changed how I pray. It changed how I lead. It changed how I show up in my marriage, with my children, with the men I mentor. Because a man who is no longer performing for God has nothing to prove to anyone else either.

You are not your performance.

You are not your provision.

You are not the image of strength you have been trying to protect.

You are a man. Loved before you proved anything. Valuable before you earned anything. Enough before you accomplished anything.

Put the scoreboard down.

You were never playing that game to begin with.

• • •

REFLECT

1. Draw the image of a "real man" you have been measuring yourself against. Where did that image come from — and who actually gave it to you?
2. Name one expectation you are carrying right now that is crushing you. Is it actually from God — or did you build it yourself?
3. What would you do differently this week if you genuinely believed your worth was already settled?

CHAPTER 7

The Wounds We Don't Name

Every man carries wounds—some obvious, some hidden, some healed, and some still bleeding beneath the surface. These wounds come from experiences that marked us, moments that shaped us, and relationships that left impressions deeper than we realized. Some wounds come from childhood, others from adulthood. Some come from people we trusted, others from situations we never saw coming. And while time may dull the memory, it rarely heals the wound on its own. Healing requires honesty, and honesty requires naming what hurts us.

Most men struggle to name their wounds because we were never taught the language of emotional truth. We learned to push through pain, not process it. We learned to bury disappointment, not confront it. We learned to silence fear, not understand it. And we learned to pretend we were fine, even when something inside us was breaking. Over time, this silence becomes a way of life. We convince ourselves that ignoring the wound is the same as healing it. But the word reminds us that truth begins with acknowledging what we've been carrying.

Some wounds come from words spoken over us—words that questioned our worth, criticized our identity, or diminished our potential. A boy who grows up hearing he is "not enough" often becomes a man who spends his life trying to prove that he is. A boy who is told to "stop crying" becomes a man who doesn't know how to express emotion. A boy who is shamed for being sensitive becomes a man who hides his tenderness behind a hardened exterior. These wounds don't disappear with age; they simply mature with us.

Other wounds come from absence—the absence of affirmation, the absence of emotional safety, the absence of a father's presence, or the absence of someone who should have protected us. Absence can wound just as deeply as action. A man who grows up without emotional support may become an adult who doesn't know how to ask for help. A man who never received affection may struggle to give it. A man who never felt seen may spend his life trying to earn visibility. Proverbs 13:12 says, "*Hope deferred makes the heart sick*," and many men carry a quiet sickness of the heart from hopes that were never fulfilled.

Some wounds come from betrayal—moments when trust was broken, loyalty was violated, or love was mishandled. Betrayal leaves a mark that is difficult to articulate. It creates a fear of vulnerability, a hesitation to trust, and a tendency to keep people at a distance. Even when a man forgives, the wound may linger, shaping how he relates to others. But that lingering ache is exactly where God meets you. He comes close to the tender places, the cracks left behind by people who should have handled your heart with care. He moves toward the parts of you that still hurt, and that is where He does some of His deepest work.

And then there are the wounds we inflict on ourselves—mistakes we made, decisions we regret, seasons we wish we could rewrite. These wounds often carry the heaviest shame because they remind us of our humanity. A man may forgive others easily but struggle to forgive himself. He may carry guilt long after God has offered grace. He may punish himself emotionally for years because he believes he deserves the pain. But Romans 8:1 declares, "*There is now no condemnation for those who are in Christ Jesus*," reminding us that shame is not God's language.

It's an invitation to breathe, to pause long enough to notice the weight you've been carrying. Not to reopen old pain, but to understand where it came from. Not to assign blame, but to let light in. Not to remain stuck, but to take a step toward healing. Because the wounds we never name quietly shape the battles we keep fighting alone.

Some of the deepest wounds a man carries are the ones he has learned to normalize. They become part of his emotional landscape—familiar, predictable, and quietly influential. A man may not even recognize them as wounds anymore; he simply calls them "how I am." But unhealed wounds have a way of shaping how we think, how we love, how we trust, and how we respond to life. They influence our reactions, our relationships, and even our faith. Proverbs 4:23 reminds us to "*guard your heart, for everything you do flows from it*," yet many men guard their hearts not from danger, but from healing.

One of the most common unspoken wounds is the wound of not being enough. This wound often begins in childhood but follows a man into adulthood like a shadow. It shows up in the pressure to perform, the fear of failure, and the constant need to prove oneself. A man may achieve great things yet still feel inadequate. He may be admired by others yet still feel unseen. He may be loved deeply yet still feel unworthy. This wound is subtle but powerful, and it often drives a man to exhaustion. But Scripture offers a counter-truth: "My grace is sufficient for you, for My power is made perfect in weakness" (2 Corinthians 12:9). God's sufficiency is not a reward for perfection—it is a gift for the wounded.

Another wound many men carry is the wound of disappointment—disappointment in themselves, in others, or in life itself. These disappointments accumulate over time: dreams that didn't unfold the way we hoped, relationships that didn't last, opportunities that slipped away, or seasons where we felt overlooked. A man may not talk about these disappointments, but they sit quietly in his heart, shaping his expectations of the future. He may become cautious, guarded, or hesitant to hope again. Yet this is the very place God loves to step in. He heals the brokenhearted and tends to wounds no one else can see, which means disappointment is not the end of the story—it is the place where healing can begin.

Some wounds come from comparison, a silent thief that steals joy and distorts identity. A man may compare his success, his family, his finances, or his spiritual life to others and feel like he is always falling short. Comparison creates insecurity, and insecurity creates isolation. It convinces a man that he must hide his struggles because everyone else seems to be doing better. But comparison is a lie—it measures our worth by someone else's journey instead of God's purpose for our own. Galatians 6:4 encourages us to "*examine our own work*," reminding us that our value is not found in how we measure up to others, but in how faithfully we walk our own path.

There are also wounds of unprocessed grief—losses that were never mourned, transitions that were never acknowledged, and changes that were never emotionally processed. Men often move quickly past grief because they feel responsible for holding others together. They become the strong one, the steady one, the one who doesn't fall apart. But grief that is never expressed becomes grief that is never healed. Jesus Himself said, "*Blessed are those who mourn, for they shall be comforted*" (Matthew 5:4), reminding us that mourning is not a sign of weakness—it is a pathway to comfort.

And then there are the wounds of silence, the things we never said, the emotions we never expressed, the truths we never voiced. Silence can feel safe, but it can also become a prison. A man may keep quiet to avoid conflict, to protect others, or to keep peace, but silence often deepens the wound instead of healing it. God invites us into honesty, not performance. The Psalms are filled with raw, unfiltered emotion—fear, anger, sorrow, confusion, hope. They remind us that God can handle our truth, even when we struggle to handle it ourselves.

This is not about reopening old wounds for the sake of pain. It is about recognizing that healing begins with naming what hurts us. It is about understanding that God cannot heal what we refuse to acknowledge. And it is about embracing the truth that the wounds we hide are often the very places where God wants to bring restoration.

Some wounds stay hidden because a man learns to function around them. He builds routines, responsibilities, and roles that allow him to keep moving without ever addressing what's hurting beneath the surface. From the outside, he appears steady—working, providing, showing up—but inside, there are places he avoids because he's afraid of what he might feel if he slows down long enough to look. These unaddressed wounds don't disappear.

One of the most common hidden wounds is the fear of abandonment. This fear doesn't always come from dramatic events; sometimes it comes from subtle patterns—emotional distance from a parent, inconsistency from a caregiver, or relationships where love felt conditional. A man who carries this wound may struggle to trust fully. He may keep people at arm's length, not because he doesn't care, but because he fears being left. He may sabotage closeness without realizing why. And even in healthy relationships, he may feel a quiet anxiety that things could fall apart at any moment. Yet God speaks directly to this fear: "*I will never leave you nor forsake you*" (Hebrews 13:5). Divine presence becomes the anchor human inconsistency could never provide.

Another wound many men carry is the wound of being misunderstood. This wound forms when a man feels unseen or unheard—when his intentions are questioned, his emotions dismissed, or his efforts overlooked. Over time, he may stop trying to explain himself. He may retreat inward, believing that no one truly understands him. This creates a loneliness that is difficult to articulate. Even surrounded by people, he feels isolated. Even loved, he feels unknown. But Scripture reminds us that God understands us completely: "*You perceive my thoughts from afar*" (Psalm 139:2). There is comfort in knowing that even when people miss the deeper layers of who we are, God never does.

Some wounds come from seasons of failure—moments when a man fell short of his own expectations or the expectations of others. These failures may be moral, relational, financial, or spiritual. And while failure is a universal human experience, many men internalize it as identity. They begin to see themselves not as men who failed, but as failures. This distorted self-view becomes a barrier to growth, intimacy, and purpose. Yet Scripture offers a different lens: "*Though the righteous fall seven times, they rise again*" (Proverbs 24:16). Falling is not the end; refusing to rise is. God's grace is not weakened by our failures—it is revealed through them.

There are also wounds tied to shame—deep, lingering feelings that something is fundamentally wrong with us. Shame is different from guilt. Guilt says, "I did something wrong." Shame says, "I am something wrong." Shame convinces a man to hide, to withdraw, to pretend. It whispers that if people knew the real him, they would reject him. But shame loses its power when brought into the light. Scripture declares, "*Those who look to Him are radiant; their faces are never covered with shame*" (Psalm 34:5). God does not expose us to humiliate us; He reveals truth to heal us.

And then there are wounds tied to identity—questions about who we are, what we're worth, and whether we matter. These wounds often form early but echo throughout adulthood. A man may achieve success yet still feel empty. He may receive praise yet still feels insecure. He may be surrounded by people yet still feel insignificant. Identity wounds are powerful because they shape every other part of life. But God speaks directly to this ache when he says, "*Since you are precious and honored in My sight, and because I love you*" (Isaiah 43:4). Identity rooted in divine love is the only identity strong enough to heal the fractures left by human experience.

Naming these wounds is not about dwelling on the past. It is about understanding the forces that shaped us so we can finally move forward with clarity and freedom. Healing begins when a man stops running from what hurt him and starts allowing God to meet him in those hidden places.

Healing begins when a man finally gives himself permission to stop pretending he is unhurt. That permission is often the hardest step, because it requires courage—not the kind of courage that charges into battle, but the quieter courage that sits still long enough to face what has been avoided. Many men fear that if they ever slow down and look inward, the pain will overwhelm them. But the truth is, unacknowledged wounds already overwhelm us—they just do it silently. And here is what I want you to hear: you do not have to become strong before God will come near. He does not stand back waiting for you to fix yourself first. He moves toward you in the very places you feel most fragile, most ashamed, most afraid—the places you were sure had to be hidden. That is exactly where He meets a man.

One of the most transformative moments in a man's life is when he realizes he doesn't have to heal alone. For years, many of us believed that emotional pain was something we had to manage privately. We learned to keep our struggles hidden, to protect others from our truth, and to carry our wounds like secret burdens. But healing rarely happens in isolation. God often uses people—trusted friends, mentors, spouses, counselors—to help us uncover what we've buried. Ecclesiastes 4:9–10 reminds us that "*two are better than one… if either of them falls, one can help the other up.*" Healing is not a sign of weakness; it is a sign of wisdom.

Some wounds require time. Others require truth. And some require forgiveness—sometimes toward others, sometimes toward ourselves. Forgiveness does not erase the past, but it loosens the grip the past has on us. It frees the heart from bitterness, resentment, and self-punishment. It opens the door for God to restore what was broken. A man who forgives is not excusing what happened; he is choosing not to let the wound define him.

There is also a kind of healing that comes from naming what we need. Many men have spent their lives giving—giving strength, giving support, giving stability—without ever learning how to receive. But healing requires receiving. Receiving comfort. Receiving understanding. Receiving grace. Receiving love. Receiving God's presence in the places we've kept hidden. Jesus invited the weary and burdened to come to Him, not because they were weak, but because they were human. Healing begins when a man stops trying to be his own savior.

As wounds begin to heal, something remarkable happens: the very places that once felt like sources of shame become sources of strength. A man who has faced his wounds becomes more compassionate, more grounded, more emotionally present. He becomes a safer place for others. He becomes more aware of his own heart and more attentive to the hearts of those he loves. He becomes a man who leads not from perfection, but from authenticity. And authenticity is far more powerful than the illusion of invulnerability.

The wounds we don't name often shape us the most. But the wounds we bring into the light become the places where God does His deepest work. Healing is not about erasing the past; it is about reclaiming the parts of us that pain tried to steal. It is about allowing God to rewrite the story—not by removing the scars, but by transforming what they mean. Scars are not signs of weakness; they are signs of survival. They are reminders that we endured, that we grew, and that God carried us through.

You are not defined by what hurts you.

You are not trapped by what you never said.

You are not bound to the wounds you've carried in silence.

You are a man God sees, God knows, and God heals.

And the journey toward wholeness begins the moment you decide that your heart deserves that healing.

• • •

REFLECT

1. What is a wound you have been carrying but have never named out loud?
2. Which type of wound—inadequacy, disappointment, comparison, grief, shame—resonates most?
3. What would it look like to bring that wound to God instead of hiding it?

CHAPTER 8

When a Man Finally Gets Honest

There comes a moment in a man's life when pretending no longer works. He reaches a point where the weight of silence, the pressure of expectations, and the wounds he has carried for years collide with the truth he has been avoiding. That moment is rarely loud. It doesn't always come through crisis or collapse. Sometimes it arrives quietly — during a late-night drive, a conversation that hits deeper than expected, or a moment alone when the noise finally settles and the heart speaks up. And when it does, a man realizes that honesty is not a threat to his strength — it is the doorway to his freedom.

For years, many men have been conditioned to hide their inner world. We learned early that vulnerability could be misunderstood, that emotions could be judged, and that honesty could be used against us. So, we built walls — strong ones. We learned to smile when we were hurting, to stay busy when we were overwhelmed, and to keep moving when our souls were begging us to slow down. We convinced ourselves that silence was safer than truth. But silence has a cost. Psalm 32:3 describes it plainly: "*When I kept silent, my bones wasted away.*" A man can function while hiding, but he cannot flourish.

I know this not as a theory. I know it as a man who hid for a long time — and paid the price for it.

THE MOMENT I STOPPED PRETENDING

I want to tell you something I have not always found easy to say out loud. There was a season of my life when I was broken in ways I would not admit to anyone. Not to my family. Not to the people I served alongside in ministry. Not even to God in any real, honest way. I would pray, but my prayers were polished. I would show up, but my showing up was performance. I was carrying the weight of a marriage that was fracturing, the grief of no longer being present daily in my daughter's life, the private shame of decisions I could not take back, and the growing fear that I had failed at the things that mattered most — and I was doing all of it alone, behind a face that said everything was fine.

What made the grief of that season so heavy was the knowledge that my choices had consequences for someone I loved more than my own life. Every father who has experienced the pain of not tucking his child in at night, of missing the ordinary moments that become extraordinary in hindsight, knows the particular weight of that regret. I carried it quietly, the way men do, and it pressed on me in ways I did not know how to name.

I remember the specific moment honesty finally broke through. It was not dramatic. There were no bright lights or thunderclaps. I was alone, and I was tired in a way that sleep could not touch, and for the first time in longer than I could measure, I stopped performing even for myself. I sat with the truth. The full weight of it. The mistakes I had made. The people I had hurt without meaning to and some I had hurt because I was too proud to admit I was struggling. The version of myself I had been holding up that was increasingly different from the man I actually was.

And I said to God — not with eloquence, not with the language of a minister — I said, "I have made a mess of some of this. I am sorry. And I don't know how to fix it."

That was my moment of honesty. And it was the most important thing I had said in years.

I want to be clear about what I am not saying. I am not saying my mistakes were small or that the people affected by them didn't carry real wounds because of my choices. They did. Some of those wounds took time to heal. Some required forgiveness I had to ask for humbly, without guarantee that it would be given. I live with a genuine regret about the ways my silence, my pride, and my unwillingness to be honest earlier caused pain to people I love. That regret is not something I perform for effect. It is something I carry with sobriety and with a commitment to be a different man going forward.

But here is what I also know — and this is where gratitude takes over from regret: God did not leave me in that moment of honesty empty-handed. He met me there. Not with condemnation. Not with a list of everything I had done wrong. He met me with the quiet, steady presence of a Father who had been waiting — not impatiently, not with frustration, but with the kind of patient love that doesn't keep score. And in that meeting, something began to shift inside me that I had not been able to manufacture through all my years of trying to be strong enough on my own.

That is grace. And I do not use that word lightly. I use it because I have experienced it in a way that I could not have deserved and cannot fully explain — only receive with gratitude.

WHAT HONESTY ACTUALLY REQUIRES

Honesty begins with admitting what we feel — not what we think we should feel, but what is actually happening inside. Many men struggle with this because they were never given permission to name their emotions. They were taught to be logical, not vulnerable; decisive, not reflective; strong, not expressive. But emotional honesty is not weakness — it is wisdom. It is the courage to acknowledge reality so that healing can begin.

Jesus modeled this kind of honesty in Gethsemane when He said, "*My soul is overwhelmed with sorrow to the point of death*" (Matthew 26:38). If the Son of

God could speak openly about His emotional state, then surely men today can learn to do the same.

There is a unique power in the moment a man finally tells the truth — to himself first, and then to others. Truth breaks the illusion that he must carry everything alone. Truth dismantles the lie that he is the only one struggling. Truth exposes the fear that has kept him silent. And truth opens the door for God to meet him in ways he has never experienced before. John 8:32 says, "*You will know the truth, and the truth will set you free.*" Freedom doesn't begin with strength. It begins with honesty.

But honesty is not just about acknowledging pain. It is also about admitting desires, hopes, disappointments, and longings. Many men have buried their dreams because life demanded survival instead of vision. They buried their joy because responsibility took priority. They buried their voices because they didn't want to cause conflict. They buried their needs because they believed they didn't matter. But buried things don't disappear — they simply wait. And when a man gets honest, those buried parts of him begin to rise again.

Honesty also requires confronting the stories we tell ourselves. Stories like "I'm fine," "I don't need help," "I can handle it," or "It's not that deep." These stories feel safe, but they keep us stuck. They keep us distant from the people who love us. They keep us disconnected from our own hearts. Psalm 51:6 says, "*You desire truth in the inward parts,*" reminding us that God is not after polished performance — He is after authenticity.

THE SPECIFIC LIES I BELIEVED

I want to go a step further here, because I think it matters. It is one thing to speak about the lies men believe in the abstract. It is another to name the ones I personally carried, because when I hear another man name his specific lies, something in me recognizes my own. So here are some of mine:

I believed that if I admitted I was struggling, I would lose the respect of the people who depended on me. So, I performed strength I did not have.

I believed that my mistakes disqualified me — that a man who had failed the way I had failed was not the kind of man God could use or restore. So, I carried shame quietly, like a sentence I was still serving.

I believed that asking for help was the same as burdening people. So, I kept my needs to myself and called it consideration.

I believed that if I could just hold everything together long enough, I could fix the damage quietly and no one would have to know how bad it had gotten. So, I tried to manage what I should have surrendered.

Every one of those beliefs was wrong. Every one of them kept me in a prison of my own construction. And every one of them began to lose its power the moment I stopped feeding them with silence and started bringing them into the light.

WHAT SHIFTS WHEN A MAN GETS HONEST

When a man finally gets honest, something shifts. His shoulders relax. His breathing deepens. His heart softens. His relationships open. His prayers become real. And for the first time in a long time, he feels like he is no longer running from himself.

Honesty also changes how a man handles conflict. Instead of shutting down, lashing out, or withdrawing, he begins to speak from a place of clarity rather than fear. He can say, "That hurt me," or "I need a moment," or "I'm not okay right now," without feeling like he is losing control. Ephesians 4:25 encourages us to "*speak truthfully to one another*" — not to create tension, but to create healing. Truth spoken with humility becomes a tool for restoration.

One of the most surprising gifts of honesty is what it does to a man's relationship with himself. The harsh self-criticism begins to soften. The internal pressure to perform begins to ease. The fear of being found out begins to fade. He no longer has to hide behind strength he doesn't feel or confidence he doesn't have. He can acknowledge his humanity without shame. He can admit his needs without fear. Psalm 51:17 says, "*A broken and contrite heart You, God, will not despise.*" God is drawn to honesty, not perfection.

And perhaps the most profound shift happens in a man's relationship with God. When he stops filtering his prayers and starts speaking from the heart, his faith becomes more authentic. He no longer feels the need to impress God with spiritual language or hide his struggles behind religious routine. He comes honestly — tired, hopeful, wounded, grateful, confused, longing. And God meets him there. Psalm 145:18 promises, "*The Lord is near to all who call on Him in truth.*" Truth becomes the meeting place between a man and his Father.

THE FREEDOM ON THE OTHER SIDE

I want to tell you what I found on the other side of honesty, because I think men need to hear it from someone who has been there.

I found that the people who truly loved me did not leave when I finally told the truth. They drew closer. The vulnerability I had spent years protecting myself from turned out to be the very thing that allowed real connection to happen — the kind that doesn't depend on me having everything together. What I thought would push people away actually invited them in.

I found that God was not surprised by anything I brought to Him. Not my failures. Not my regrets. Not the specific places where I had let people down. He already knew. He was not waiting for my confession so He could be informed — He was waiting for it so that I could be free.

I found that the mistakes I had made, as real and as costly as some of them were, were not the final word on my story. God is a God of redemption, not just forgiveness. He doesn't simply wipe the slate — He builds something new on it.

And He proved that to me in a way I did not see coming.

Years after my divorce, after the season of honest reckoning and the slow work of healing, God brought a woman into my life who would become my wife. Shannon. And with her came something I had not dared to believe was still possible for a man who had failed the way I had failed — a new family. Three more children. Two sons and another daughter. Not a replacement for what had been broken, but a restoration that exceeded what I thought I had lost. God did not give me back what I had — He gave me more than I deserved, and He did it through the very vulnerability and honesty that I had spent years avoiding.

I tell you this because I need you to understand something: the path through your honest moment is not just survival. It is abundance. It is God showing up not merely to patch the wound, but to grow something in that ground that could not have grown any other way. The man I became through that season of brokenness was a man capable of loving Shannon with a depth and honesty I simply did not have before. I was prepared — not despite the failure, but through it.

That is not something I take lightly. That is grace upon grace. And I am grateful in a way that has no bottom.

I am grateful for that moment of honesty. More than I can adequately say.

Whatever it costs a man to be honest — and it can cost something real, make no mistake — the weight he lays down in that moment is worth every bit of what vulnerability requires. Because you were not built to carry all of this alone. You were built for truth. And truth, when you finally speak it, has a way of setting things in motion that years of silence never could.

When a man finally gets honest, he steps into a new kind of strength — one rooted not in pressure, but in peace; not in performance, but in presence; not in fear, but in faith. He becomes a man who can breathe deeply, love fully, and walk confidently in the truth of who God created him to be.

And that kind of man is not just free.

He is whole.

• • •

REFLECT

1. What is the truth you have been most afraid to say out loud — to yourself, to God, or to someone you trust? What would it cost you to say it? What might it free you from?
2. Name one specific lie you have believed about yourself that has kept you hidden. What does Scripture say in response to that lie?

3. Think of a relationship where your silence or pretending has created distance. What is one honest thing you could say that might begin to close that gap?

CHAPTER 9

Learning to Feel Again

There comes a point in a man's journey where honesty opens a door he didn't expect. Once he stops pretending, once he stops hiding, once he finally tells the truth about what he feels, something begins to awaken inside him—something he may not have felt in years. It's subtle at first, almost unfamiliar. But it's real. It's the beginning of learning to feel again.

For many men, emotional numbness becomes a way of life. Not because they don't care, but because caring has cost them something in the past. They learned to shut down to survive. They learned to disconnect to function. They learned to silence their hearts because their hearts felt too heavy to carry. Over time, numbness becomes normal. A man may not even realize he's numb—he just knows he doesn't feel much anymore. Not joy. Not sadness. Not excitement. Not grief. Just... steady. Flat. Controlled. But Scripture reminds us that God created us with a full emotional range: "*He heals the brokenhearted and binds up their wounds*" (Psalm 147:3). Healing assumes feelings.

HOW NUMBNESS BEGINS

Numbness often begins with pain. A man experiences something that overwhelms him—loss, betrayal, disappointment, failure—and instead of processing it, he shuts down. He tells himself, "I'm fine," because the alternative feels too risky. He keeps moving because stopping feels dangerous. He stays busy because stillness might expose what he's been avoiding. And slowly, the heart that once felt deeply begins to retreat. What started as protection becomes a prison.

But numbness doesn't just block pain—it blocks everything. It blocks joy. It blocks connection. It blocks intimacy. It blocks hope. A man may function well on the outside, but inside he feels disconnected from the world around him. He may love his family deeply yet feel distant. He may believe in God sincerely yet feel spiritually dry. He may have blessings all around him yet feel unable to fully experience them. Proverbs 14:13 captures this tension: "*Even in laughter the heart may ache.*" Outward expressions don't always reflect inward reality.

Learning to feel again begins with permission—permission to acknowledge what's happening inside without judgment or shame. Many men have never been given that permission. They were taught to "man up," to "shake it off," to "push through." But emotional suppression is not strength; it is survival. And survival is not the same as living. When a man gives himself permission to feel, he begins to reconnect with the parts of himself he thought were gone.

This awakening often starts small. A moment of unexpected emotion. A memory that stirs something. A conversation that hits deeper than usual. A worship song that touches a place he didn't know was still tender. These moments are not signs of weakness—they are signs of life. Ezekiel 36:26 speaks to this beautifully: "I will give you a new heart and put a new spirit in you; I will remove your heart of stone and give you a heart of flesh." God specializes in restoring what has grown numb.

As a man begins to feel again, he may experience emotions he hasn't touched in years. Some will be painful. Some will be beautiful. Some will be confusing. But all of them are part of the healing process. Feeling is not the enemy. Feeling is the evidence that the heart is waking up.

And a waking heart is a hopeful heart.

As a man begins to awaken emotionally, he often discovers that feeling again is both beautiful and unsettling. After years of numbness, emotions can feel intense—sometimes too intense. Joy feels brighter. Sadness feels heavier. Anger feels sharper. Compassion feels deeper. Everything feels more alive. And while this awakening is a sign of healing, it can also feel unfamiliar, even uncomfortable. Many men wonder, "Is something wrong with me?" when something is finally becoming right.

GRIEF RESURFACES

For me, this awakening collided with a grief I had never fully allowed myself to feel. Losing my daughter Brittany was a pain so deep, so disorienting, that I didn't know how to process it. I loved her with everything in me, and when she was gone, something inside me went quiet. I didn't have the tools to grieve her properly. I didn't know how to sit with that kind of heartbreak. So, I did what many men do—I kept moving. I stayed busy. I stayed strong. I stayed functional. But inside, I was numb.

And before I could even catch my breath, I lost my brother Manuel. Another blow. Another wound. Another piece of my heart torn away. I miss them both deeply—more than words can express. And the truth is, I wish I had taken the time to really grieve them. I wish I had given myself permission to feel the weight of those losses instead of burying them beneath responsibility and routine. I knew God was near. I preached it to others all the time. But knowing it and letting myself live in it were two different things—and I couldn't bring myself to fall apart, not even in His presence, not even when that was exactly what I needed to do. I just didn't know how to let myself be brokenhearted.

Grief has a way of resurfacing when the heart begins to wake up. Not to torment us, but to heal us. When I finally slowed down enough to feel again, the grief I had avoided for years rose to the surface—not to drown me, but to free me. I realized that numbness had protected me for a season, but it had also kept me from honoring the depth of my love for Brittany and Manuel. Feeling again meant remembering them—not just the pain of losing them, but the beauty of who they were.

Another emotion that often returns in this awakening is anger. Not the explosive kind, but the quiet anger that comes from realizing how long we've carried pain alone. Anger at the expectations placed on us. Anger at the silence we were taught. Anger at the wounds we never named. Anger at ourselves for not knowing how to do better. This anger is not sinful—it is informative. It reveals where boundaries were crossed, where needs were ignored, and where healing is needed. Ephesians 4:26 says, "*Be angry and do not sin,*" reminding us that anger itself is not the problem; it is what we do with it that matters.

As emotions return, compassion often returns with them—toward others and toward ourselves. We begin to see people differently. We listen more deeply. We notice things we once overlooked. We become more patient, more understanding, more present. This compassion is not weakness; it is strength softened by truth. Colossians 3:12 calls us to "*clothe yourselves with compassion,*" as a reflection of God's heart for us.

There is also a surprising tenderness that appears. A man who once felt hardened by life begins to feel again—toward his spouse, his children, his friends, and even toward God. He may find himself moved by things that never touched him before: a moment of worship, a heartfelt conversation, a memory, a simple act of kindness. This tenderness is not a threat to his masculinity; it is evidence of his humanity. It is the heart of flesh God promised in Ezekiel 36:26 beginning to beat again.

But with this awakening comes vulnerability. Feeling again means risking again. It means opening the heart to joy and disappointment, connection and conflict, hope, and uncertainty. Many men fear this vulnerability because they associate it with pain. But vulnerability is not exposure, it is openness. It is the willingness to live fully rather than safely. It is the courage to let God and others into the places that once felt off-limits.

As a man learns to feel again, he may experience moments of overwhelm. That is normal. Healing is not linear. Some days the heart feels open; other days it feels guarded. Some moments feel freeing; others feel frightening. But every step toward emotional honesty is a step toward wholeness. Psalm 30:5 reminds us, "*Weeping may endure for a night, but joy comes in the morning.*" Emotional awakening may begin with tears, but it leads to joy.

Feeling again is not about becoming emotional—it is about becoming alive.

As a man begins to feel again, he often discovers that emotions don't return in neat, organized categories. They come in waves—unexpected, uninvited, and sometimes overwhelming. A memory can surface out of nowhere. A song can stir something long buried. A quiet moment can open a door he didn't know was still locked. This is not regression; it is resurrection. It is the heart waking up after years of silence. Psalm 30:11 captures this beautifully: "*You turned my mourning into dancing; You removed my sackcloth and clothed me with joy.*" But before joy comes dancing, mourning must be acknowledged.

One of the most surprising parts of emotional awakening is how grief resurfaces—not to torment, but to heal. When I began to feel again, I found myself revisiting the losses I had pushed down for years. I have been in jobs that I really loved, only to discover that I was being terminated. It leaves a deep wound when you do not see it coming. It left a wound so deep that numbness felt like the only way to survive. I didn't know how to hold that much sorrow, so I didn't. I kept moving. I kept working. I kept functioning. But when my heart began to thaw, the grief I had avoided came back—not as punishment, but as invitation. It was as if God was saying, "Let's finally walk through this together."

Emotional awakening often brings clarity. A man begins to see how his unprocessed pain shaped his reactions, his relationships, and even his faith. He realizes that the distance he felt from others wasn't because he didn't love them—it was because he didn't know how to let himself feel. He realizes that the heaviness he carried wasn't a lack of strength—it was a lack of space to grieve. He realizes that the numbness he lived with wasn't a flaw—it was a survival strategy. And survival strategies are not meant to become permanent homes.

Another part of learning to feel again is rediscovering joy. Not the loud, celebratory kind, but the quiet joy that sneaks up on you. The joy of a peaceful morning. The joy of a meaningful conversation. The joy of remembering someone you lost—not with only pain, but with gratitude for who they were. This kind of joy doesn't erase grief; it sits beside it. Psalm 126:5 says, "*Those who sow with tears will reap with songs of joy.*" Tears and joy are not opposites—they are companions.

As emotions return, a man may also feel a renewed sense of spiritual sensitivity. Worship hits differently. Scripture feels more personal. Prayer becomes more honest. He begins to sense God's presence not just in strength, but in vulnerability. He realizes that God was never asking him to be emotionally numb—He was inviting him to bring his whole heart, even the broken parts. The Psalms show us this over and over: David cried, questioned, lamented, rejoiced, and worshiped with raw honesty. God never turned him away.

Feeling again also brings a deeper awareness of others. A man who reconnects with his own heart becomes more attuned to the hearts around him. He notices pain he once overlooked. He listens with more patience. He responds with more compassion. He becomes a safer place for others because he has learned to be a safer place for himself. This is the fruit of emotional awakening—not just internal healing, but relational transformation.

But the most profound part of learning to feel again is the realization that emotions are not enemies, they are indicators. They reveal where healing is needed. They reveal where love is present. They reveal where boundaries were crossed. They reveal where God is working. They reveal where the heart is waking up.

And a waking heart is a courageous heart.

As a man continues learning to feel again, he begins to realize that emotional awakening is not about becoming someone different—it is about returning to who he truly is. The heart he thought was gone was never gone;

it was simply buried under years of responsibility, pain, silence, and survival. When God begins to breathe life into those hidden places, the man who emerges is not weaker—he is more whole. Psalm 23:3 says, "*He restores my soul,*" and restoration is exactly what begins to unfold.

This restoration also brings a new kind of courage. Not the courage to fight battles on the outside, but the courage to face the battles within. The courage to sit with grief instead of running from it. The courage to acknowledge regret without drowning in it. The courage to remember loved ones—like Brittany and Manuel—not with numbness, but with tenderness. The courage to say, "I miss them," and let the tears come if they need to. Psalm 56:8 reminds us that God puts our tears in His bottle, meaning none of them are wasted. Every tear is seen. Every ache is known.

As the heart heals, a man begins to reconnect with parts of himself he thought were lost forever. He rediscovers laughter—not the polite kind, but the deep, genuine kind that rises from a place of freedom. He rediscovers gratitude—not forced, but natural. He rediscovers hope—not fragile, but steady. He rediscovers the ability to love with depth, to listen with empathy, and to show up with presence. These are not new qualities—they are restored ones.

This emotional awakening also transforms a man's relationship with God. He begins to approach God as someone who is held, someone who can finally set the weight down. He prays from a place of honesty now, bringing his real self instead of his rehearsed one. He carries his wounds into the light, and there he discovers something that changes everything: God is drawn to his humanity. The honest, unguarded, fully-known version of him is exactly the version God wants. And when a man dares to come that openly, he finds God already there, already near, ready to meet him in the truth. That is where healing begins.

As a man learns to feel again, he also learns to live again. He becomes more present in his relationships. He becomes more aware of beauty. He becomes more open to joy. He becomes more anchored in peace. He becomes more connected to his own story—not as something to escape, but as something God is redeeming. The numbness that once protected him is replaced by a strength that is softer, deeper, and more resilient.

And the man who once lived numb begins to live awake.

Awake to God.

Awake to himself.

Awake to love.

Awake to life.

• • •

REFLECT

1. What emotions have you been avoiding, and what might they be trying to tell you?
2. Has there been a loss or grief you never fully processed? What would it take to begin?
3. What is one small step you can take this week to reconnect with your own heart?

CHAPTER 10

Learning to Trust Again

Let me tell you what a man who has stopped trusting looks like — because he doesn't look like what you might expect. He doesn't walk around, obviously guarded. He doesn't announce that he's been hurt. He shows up. He functions. He does his job, comes home, maintains his relationships. From the outside he looks fine. Better than fine, maybe. Competent. Self-sufficient. Steady.

But watch him more carefully.

When someone gets too close, he finds a reason to create distance. Not dramatically — just a step back. A change of subject. A little less disclosed than last time. He is present in conversations but controls the depth of them. He is capable of warmth but not quite available for it. He will give you access to most of himself, but there are rooms in the house he keeps locked, and he does it so naturally that neither of you notices.

That was me for a long time.

And here is what I want you to understand about that version of a man: he is not cold. He is not unloving. He is not indifferent. He is protecting himself the only way he knows how — with a management strategy that got built in seasons when being open cost him something real.

HOW TRUST BREAKS IN THE FIRST PLACE

Trust doesn't usually break in one dramatic moment. Sometimes it does — a betrayal, a loss, something sudden that reshapes everything. But more often it erodes. Slowly. Incrementally. Through accumulated experiences that teach a man the same lesson over and over until he stops needing to be taught it anymore.

He opens up to someone, and it is used against him later. He is vulnerable with a woman and she leaves. He trusts a leader and gets burned. He prays with real desperation in a hard season, and the hard season doesn't end the way he asked. He reaches out for help, and the response is either awkward or absent. None of these things individually would do much. Together, over years, they become a quiet conviction: it is safer not to depend on anything you can't control.

I built that conviction brick by brick.

I had seasons where I trusted people with things that mattered to me and came back empty. I had relationships where I tried to be honest and it cost me more than hiding would have. I had a season where my life fell apart despite everything I had tried to do right, and sitting in the rubble of that I had very real, very raw questions for God that I did not voice out loud for a long time because I wasn't sure what it meant that I had them.

What do you do when you are not sure you can trust the one Person, you're supposed to be able to trust completely?

You don't have to answer that question right now. But if it lives somewhere in you — if you have ever had a season where God felt absent or silent or confusing, where you did the right things and life fell apart anyway, where you prayed and felt like the ceiling — I need you to know that is not a faith problem. That is a human being in pain, asking honest questions. And God is not offended by honest questions. He is drawn to them.

THE DIFFERENCE BETWEEN PROTECTION AND PRISON

There is a version of self-protection that is wisdom. You do not have to trust everyone. You do not have to be fully open with people who have not earned it. Discernment is real. Boundaries are healthy. Not every person who wants access to your interior life deserves it.

But there is another version of self-protection that becomes a prison. It is the version where you stop trusting anything you can't control. Where every relationship gets managed at arm's length. Where you are technically present but genuinely unreachable. Where you stop praying honestly because honesty feels too risky. Where the loneliness that results feels safer than the vulnerability that might relieve it.

I lived in that prison for seasons of my life. I called it strength. It was not strength. It was a wound that had hardened over time until it started to look like a wall.

The difference I eventually learned between protection and prison is this: protection keeps specific dangers out while leaving the door open for love, for God, for genuine connection. Prison keeps everything out — the dangerous and the good alike. And a man in a prison of his own making will eventually look around and realize that he is alone in a space of his own construction, and nobody put him there but him.

WHAT IT ACTUALLY TAKES TO TRUST AGAIN

I am not going to tell you that rebuilding trust is simple. It isn't. And I am not going to tell you it happens fast. It doesn't. Anyone who has had their trust broken at a deep level knows that the process of reopening to people, to life, to God, is gradual and sometimes two steps forward and one step back.

But I will tell you what made it possible for me.

The first thing was deciding that the cost of staying closed was higher than the risk of opening up. That sounds obvious but it took me a long time to get there. I had calculated — unconsciously, but thoroughly — that staying protected was the safer bet. What I had not calculated was what that protection was costing me. The relationships that couldn't grow because I wouldn't let them. The intimacy with God I was missing because I was still managing how much I brought to Him. The version of myself I was not becoming because I was too defended to be shaped.

When I finally put those costs on the table honestly, the math changed.

The second thing was starting small. Trust is not rebuilt in one large act of courage. It is rebuilt in small consistent decisions to extend a little more than you did yesterday. To tell someone one true thing about how you are actually doing. To bring one honest prayer to God — not a polished one, just a real one. To sit with uncertainty instead of immediately trying to control it.

I remember the first time I prayed with real honesty about losing Brittany. Not the composed, spiritually acceptable version of that grief — the actual grief. The anger in it. The questions in it. The places where it still didn't make sense and I didn't know what to do with that. I had been managing that prayer for a long time. When I finally stopped managing it, God met me in it in a way He had not been able to while I was still curating what I brought to Him.

That is what trust with God looks like. Not blind faith that pretends everything is fine. But honest engagement with the One who already knows what you're carrying and is waiting for you to bring it rather than manage it in private.

The third thing — and this is the one men resist most — was letting other people in. Not everyone. But someone. A trusted friend. A counselor. A brother who could hold what I was carrying without using it against me. There is something that happens in genuine human connection that cannot happen in isolation. God designed it that way on purpose. We were not built to carry our interior lives alone.

I regret the years I tried to.

I am grateful beyond words for the ones I stopped.

TRUST IS NOT CERTAINTY

I want to close this chapter with something that took me a long time to understand.

Trust is not the same as certainty. It does not mean everything will go the way you want. It does not mean you will not be hurt again. It does not mean life will be smooth or that God will always answer the way you hoped.

Trust means you believe that whatever comes, you are not facing it alone. It means you believe that the God who has been faithful in the past is the same God in the present — even when the present is hard. It means you believe that connection, even imperfect human connection, is worth the risk of it.

I have had enough of my trust proven right to know that it is worth extending again.

And so have you, if you are willing to look for it.

Your story is not over. The walls you built were not meant to be permanent. And the freedom on the other side of learning to trust again is not a small thing — it is the difference between surviving your life and actually living it.

You were built to live it.

• • •

REFLECT

1. Name a specific moment when your trust was broken. How has that moment shaped the walls you've built since? Have you ever named it out loud to anyone?
2. Identify one area — with God, with your spouse, with a friend — where you are currently protecting yourself in a way that is also keeping love out. What would one small step of openness look like?
3. What would you bring to God right now if you genuinely believed He could handle the unedited version of it?

CHAPTER 11

Learning to Receive Love

There comes a moment in a man's healing journey when he realizes that the hardest thing for him to do is not to give love—but to receive it. Most men have spent their entire lives being the strong one, the steady one, the dependable one. They know how to provide, protect, and persevere. They know how to show up for others. But when love turns toward them—when someone tries to care for them, support them, or pour into them—they often don't know what to do with it.

Receiving love requires openness, and openness requires vulnerability. And vulnerability is the very thing many men were taught to avoid. So even when love is offered freely, a man may instinctively deflect it. He may downplay compliments. He may brush off concern. He may reject help. He may hide his needs. Not because he doesn't want love, but because he doesn't know how to let it in.

For many men, this struggle is deeply personal. I know it was for me. For years, I wrestled with the belief that someone could genuinely love me for me—not for what I did, not for how strong I appeared, not for how much I carried, but for who I was at my core. That kind of love felt foreign. Unbelievable. Unsafe. So even when someone tried to love me genuinely, I questioned it. I doubted it. I waited for it to disappear. And because I didn't believe I deserved it, I often sabotaged relationships before they had a chance to grow. I pushed people away. I created distance. I found reasons to leave before they could leave me. Not because I didn't want love, but because I didn't know how to receive it.

This struggle often begins early. Many men grew up in environments where love was expressed through responsibility rather than affection. They were taught that love meant working hard, providing, staying strong, and not complaining. So, when someone tries to love them emotionally—through empathy, affirmation, or tenderness—it feels unfamiliar. It feels uncomfortable. It feels undeserved. But Scripture reminds us that love is not earned; it is given. First John 4:19 says, "*We love because He first loved us.*" God initiates love. We respond to it.

Receiving love also requires confronting the quiet belief that we are unworthy of it. Many men carry internal narratives shaped by past failures, regrets, or wounds. They think, "If people really knew me, they wouldn't love me." Or, "I've messed up too much." Or, "I don't deserve grace." These beliefs become barriers that keep love at a distance. But God's love is not based on performance—it is based on identity. Romans 8:38–39 declares that
38 "*For I am convinced that neither death nor life, neither angels nor demons, neither the present nor the future, nor any powers,*
39 neither height nor depth, nor anything else in all creation, will be able to separate us from the love of God that is in Christ Jesus our Lord."

Contemporary life reinforces this struggle. A man may be praised at work for his competence but rarely affirmed for his heart. He may be admired for his strength but rarely encouraged in his vulnerability. He may be surrounded by people yet feel emotionally unseen. So, when someone finally tries to love him deeply—whether it's a spouse, a child, a friend, or God Himself—he may not know how to receive it. He may feel exposed. He may feel unsure. He may feel like he's losing control.

Receiving love also means allowing others to show up for you. Think of the man who has always been the one others call when they need help. But when he goes through a difficult season—grief, illness, and financial strain, he struggles to let anyone support him. He insists, "I'm fine." He says, "I've got it." He pushes through alone. Not because he wants to be alone, but because he doesn't know how to let others carry him. Yet Galatians 6:2 calls us to "*carry each other's burdens*," which means love is meant to be shared, not hoarded.

Receiving love also means allowing God to love you in ways you've never experienced. Not just through blessings or answered prayers, but through comfort, presence, and grace. It means letting Him into the places you've kept hidden—the grief of divorce, or the loss of a parent. The wounds you carried silently, the emotions you buried to survive. God does not love the polished version of you; He loves the real you. The hurting you. The healing you. The becoming you.

Learning to receive love is not weakness, it is wisdom. It is the recognition that you were never meant to carry life alone. It is the courage to let others in. It is the humility to accept what you have long given but rarely received. It is the doorway to deeper healing, deeper connection, and deeper faith. When a man learns to receive love, he can finally live as a man who knows he is loved.

As a man begins learning to receive love, he often discovers that the greatest battle is not external—it is internal. Love can be right in front of him, offered sincerely and consistently, yet something inside resists it. Not because he doesn't want it, but because he doesn't trust it. He may even question the motives behind it. "Why would she love me?" "What does he see in me?" "What if they change their mind?" These questions don't come from arrogance—they come from wounds.

Many men live this same pattern without realizing it. A man may meet someone who genuinely cares for him, but the moment the relationship becomes emotionally intimate, he panics. He becomes inconsistent. He withdraws. He overthinks. He questions everything. Not because the relationship is unhealthy, but because love feels unfamiliar. Or he may be in a long-term relationship, but every time his partner expresses affection, he feels uncomfortable—almost suspicious. He wonders, "What does she want?" or "Why now?" because he has never learned to simply receive love without strings attached.

This resistance often comes from past experiences. A man who grew up without emotional affirmation may not know how to accept it as an adult. A man who was betrayed may struggle to trust affection. A man who was criticized more than he was encouraged may feel undeserving of tenderness. A man who was taught to be strong may feel weak when someone tries to care for him. These early experiences shape how he interprets love later in life.

In the world we live in, this struggle is constantly reinforced. Men are often recognized for what they do, but not for who they are. They are applauded for their work ethic, their resilience, their leadership, and their strength. Yet rarely are they affirmed for their vulnerability, their compassion, or the depth of their emotions. So, when someone tries to love them for their heart, not their performance, they don't know how to respond. It feels foreign. It feels risky. It feels like stepping into a room they were never taught how to enter.

Receiving love also requires letting go of the belief that you must be perfect to be loved. Many men carry silent shame—mistakes they made, seasons they survived, regrets they never voiced. They fear that if someone saw the full truth, the love would disappear. But real love—healthy love—does not demand perfection. It embraces humanity. It sees flaws and chooses connection anyway. First Peter 4:8 says, "Love covers a multitude of sins," not to excuse wrongdoing, but to remind us that love is bigger than our failures.

As a man learns to receive love, something begins to soften inside him. He becomes less defensive. Less guarded. Less suspicious. He begins to trust that love can be real. He begins to trust that he is worthy of it. He begins to trust that God can use love to heal places he thought were beyond repair.

And slowly, the man who once pushed love away begins to let it in.

As a man slowly learns to receive love, something begins to shift inside him. The walls he built for protection start to soften. The suspicion that once guarded his heart begins to loosen its grip. The fear that love will disappear starts to fade. This shift doesn't happen all at once—it happens in moments. Small, sacred moments where love proves itself trustworthy.

Many men live with this same internal conflict. A man may be in a healthy relationship yet constantly wait for the other shoe to drop. He may interpret a partner's silence as rejection. He may see disagreement as a sign that the relationship is falling apart. He may feel anxious when things are going well because he's not used to stability. These reactions are not signs of immaturity, they are signs of a heart that has been wounded and is learning to trust again.

Another sign of growth is when a man begins to let love challenge him. Real love doesn't just comfort—it confronts. It calls out the best in him. It invites him to grow. It asks him to be honest. It asks him to be present. It asks him to be accountable. And for a man who has spent years hiding behind strength, this can feel uncomfortable. But it is also healing. Proverbs 27:6 says, "*Faithful are the wounds of a friend,*" meaning that love sometimes speaks truth that helps us become whole.

In today's world, we see this play out in so many ways. Think of the man who has always kept his emotions guarded, but his partner gently encourages him to open up. At first, he resists. He feels exposed. But over time, he realizes that her desire for closeness is not criticism—it is love. Or the man who has always been the provider, but his wife tells him, "I don't just need your strength—I need your heart." At first, he feels inadequate. But eventually, he realizes that love is not asking him to be more, it is asking him to be real.

Receiving love also means allowing yourself to be celebrated. Many men struggle with this. Compliments make them uncomfortable. Affirmation feels strange. Appreciation feels undeserved. But learning to receive love means learning to accept the truth about who you are—not the harsh version you've believed, but the version God sees. Zephaniah 3:17 says that God "rejoices over you with singing." That means God delights in you—not because of what you do, but because of who you are.

Another layer of receiving love is learning to stay when things get uncomfortable. In the past, when love felt too close, I would retreat. I would withdraw emotionally. I would create distance. I would find reasons to sabotage relationships. I would find reasons to step back. But healing came when I learned to stay present even when my instinct was to run. When I learned to breathe through the discomfort. When I learned to trust that love wasn't trying to trap me—it was trying to heal me.

This is where many men experience breakthrough. The moment they stay instead of shutting down. The moment they speak instead of withdrawing. The moment they allow someone to comfort them instead of pretending they're fine. The moment they let God's love reach the places they once hid. These moments are not dramatic, but they are transformative.

Receiving love also changes how a man sees the people who love him. He begins to recognize their patience. Their consistency. Their grace. He sees the ways they stayed when he pushed them away. He sees the ways they believed in him when he doubted himself. He sees the ways they loved him even when he didn't know how to love himself. And that realization softens him. It humbles him. It heals him.

As a man learns to receive love, he begins to understand that love is not a threat—it is a gift. A gift that strengthens him. A gift that grounds him. A gift that restores him. A gift that reminds him that he is not alone.

One of the most profound shifts happens when a man begins to believe that love is not something he must earn. For years, I lived with the quiet pressure to prove myself worthy of love. I thought I had to be strong enough, good enough, consistent enough, spiritual enough. I thought love was a reward for performance. But real love—healthy love—does not work that way. Real love is not a paycheck; it is a gift. And gifts are received, not earned. Ephesians 2:8 reminds us that even God's love comes by grace, not by works. If God does not require perfection to love us, why do we need it of ourselves?

Receiving love also changes the way a man responds to conflict. Instead of shutting down or withdrawing, he begins to stay engaged. Instead of assuming the worst, he becomes willing to listen. Instead of interpreting correction as rejection, he begins to see it as care. Think of the man who once walked away at the first sign of tension. Now, he takes a breath and says, "Let's talk about it." That is growth. That is maturity. That is love doing its work.

Receiving love also reshapes a man's relationship with God. He no longer approaches God as someone who must hide his flaws or pretend to be strong. He comes honestly. He comes openly. He comes as a son, not a soldier. He begins to understand that God's love is not fragile, conditional, or performance-based. It is steady. It is patient. It is healing. Romans 5:8 says that God showed His love "*while we were still sinners*," meaning God loved us before we ever got it right. That truth alone can transform a man's entire identity.

And perhaps the most powerful shift is this: a man who learns to receive love stops running from it. He stops sabotaging relationships. He stops doubting every good thing. He stops assuming he is unworthy. He stops pushing people away. Instead, he leans in. He stays present. He allows himself to be seen, known, and cared for. He allows himself to be loved.

Receiving love does not make a man weak—it makes him whole. It makes him grounded. It makes him emotionally available. It makes him spiritually anchored. It makes him capable of deeper connection, deeper intimacy, and deeper purpose.

And the man who once questioned whether he was lovable becomes a man who lives loved.

• • •

REFLECT

1. When someone tries to love you, is your first instinct to receive it or deflect it?
2. What belief about yourself makes it hard for you to accept love?
3. How might your life change if you truly believed God loves you as you are?

CHAPTER 12

From Failure to Fatherhood

From Failure to Fatherhood — The Power of Forgiveness. "*Make allowance for each other's faults and forgive anyone who offends you. Remember, the Lord forgave you, so you must forgive others.*" – Colossians 3:13 (NLT)

Forgiveness is one of the most powerful tools God has given us. It has the power to release, to heal, and to transform—not only others, but ourselves. Yet for many men, forgiveness is a struggle. We hold on to offenses, sometimes for years, believing that by doing so we're somehow protecting ourselves. But in reality, we're only prolonging the pain.

Forgiveness does not mean that what happened was okay. It doesn't mean you weren't wronged or that your pain isn't valid. Forgiveness means you are choosing to release the offense, so it no longer controls you. It means you are handing the situation over to God, trusting Him to be the righteous judge.

Holding on to unforgiveness is like drinking poison and expecting the other person to die. It eats away at your joy, your peace, and your relationships. It builds walls where God wants to build bridges.

I had to walk the road of forgiveness in several areas of my life—toward those who hurt me, abandoned me, misunderstood me, and even toward myself. There were moments I wanted revenge, moments I replayed old conversations and dreamed of what I "should have said." But none of it brought peace.

Peace only came when I let go. When I released those people, not because they deserved it, but because I needed to be free. For God said in his word,

"*Instead, be kind to each other, tenderhearted, forgiving one another, just as God through Christ has forgiven you.*" – Ephesians 4:32 (NLT)

Forgiveness is not weakness—it's strength. It's not a one-time act—it's often a daily choice. You may need to forgive someone over and over until the wound no longer bleeds. And that's okay. God honors every step toward freedom.

Sometimes the hardest person to forgive is yourself. But if God can forgive you—and He has—you can learn to extend that grace to yourself. You are not your mistakes. You are not your past.

Forgiveness doesn't change the past. But it will change your future. It will open your heart to love again, to trust again, to live again.

Let forgiveness be your weapon, your shield, and your breakthrough. There is power in letting go. And in Christ, there is always grace to begin again.

There was a time when I felt like a complete failure. I felt like I was destined to spend the rest of my life as a single man. Divorce has a way of magnifying every mistake, every moment of doubt, every word spoken in anger or silence held in pain. It tore through my life like a storm, leaving wreckage I didn't know how to clear. I had to learn how to love myself again. I had to take the time to forgive myself. That may surprise some men to hear, but we can sometimes be our own worst enemy. Forgiveness frees you.

There were nights I lay awake wondering if I had lost everything that mattered. I questioned whether I had failed not just as a husband, but as a father. The guilt was overwhelming. I grieved for the family I couldn't hold together. I grieved for the version of myself that I didn't know how to fix what was broken.

But in the quiet of those lonely nights, God met me. He came with comfort; with a gentleness I didn't think I deserved and couldn't earn. He stayed close through the worst of it, sitting with me in the dark when I had nothing left to offer Him but my brokenness. I held onto His presence like a lifeline, trusting that even in my failure, even in the wreckage I couldn't clean up myself, He was already at work on something new. He was still for me. And slowly, in His nearness, I began to believe I could be whole again.

Fatherhood continued to be my priority. The arrangement changes, yes, but it doesn't vanish. I learned how to father from a distance. I learned how to be intentional with phone calls, how to text her with the words "I Love You." These things that spoke from the heart, how to show up even when it hurt. It wasn't the kind of fatherhood I envisioned, but it was no less real. And through it all, God began to rebuild my confidence—not in my perfection, but in His purpose for me as a father.

Over time, healing began to take root. My relationship with my daughter, though different, remained strong. My relationship with her mother, turned into mutual respect and the responsibility to work together to raise our daughter. I asked for forgiveness for the things that I had said and done, along with accepting my failure to love her like she should have been loved. We laughed again. We shared stories again. We began to create new memories. I thank God for the resilience of children, for their ability to forgive and love freely. She taught me just as much as I taught her—maybe more. And in her smile, I saw hope. I saw a future I could still be a part of.

Later, when I remarried, God added more children to my life. Two sons and another daughter. It wasn't a replacement, it was redemption. It was God showing me that He could multiply love, that He could restore what was lost and add even more than I expected. Loving these children has been a second chance—not only at fatherhood but at life.

Today, I walk as a man who understands that failure is part of the journey—but it doesn't define the destination. Fatherhood is not about being flawless, it's about being faithful. It's about showing up, saying "I love you," and being a safe place for your children to grow. "*Fathers, do not provoke your children to anger, but bring them up in the discipline and instruction of the Lord*" (Ephesians 6:4, ESV). That's the model I aim to live by now—not perfect, but present. Not always strong but always striving.

So, to every man who feels like he's messed up too badly to be a good father—hear me: God is not done with you. Your story is not over. You can still be the father your children need. With God's help, you can be a source of strength, wisdom, and love. Your past may have been broken, but your future can be blessed.

• • •

REFLECT

1. Am I willing to seek forgiveness where I've failed? "*If we confess our sins to him, he is faithful and just to forgive us our sins and to cleanse us from all wickedness.*" – 1 John 1:9 (NLT)
2. Am I courageous enough to forgive myself?
3. What is one relationship—with God, another person, or yourself—where forgiveness could change everything?

CHAPTER 13

Learning to Give Love Freely

Once a man learns to receive love, something remarkable begins to happen inside him. The love he once resisted, questioned, or pushed away starts to take root. It begins to soften him, steady him, and strengthen him. And as that love settles into the deeper places of his heart, he discovers a new capacity rising within him—the capacity to give love freely.

Giving love freely is quite different from giving love out of obligation. Many men have spent their entire lives giving love from a place of duty. They provided because they were supposed to. They protected because it was expected. They showed up because that's what a man does. And while those actions are noble, they often came from a place of pressure rather than presence. A man can give love with his hands while his heart is still guarded.

But when a man has learned to receive love—truly receive it—his giving changes. It becomes more authentic. More intentional. More tender. More courageous. He no longer gives love to earn approval or avoid conflict. He gives love because he is full, not because he is empty. First John 4:11 says, "*Since God so loved us, we also ought to love one another.*" Love received becomes love expressed.

It also shows up in how a man handles conflict. Instead of shutting down or withdrawing, he leans in. Instead of reacting defensively, he listens. Instead of protecting his pride, he protects the relationship. Love frees him from the need to win and empowers him to pursue peace. Proverbs 15:1 reminds us that "*a gentle answer turns away wrath*," and a man who has learned to give love freely becomes a man who can respond gently even when emotions run high.

Giving love freely also means giving love without keeping score. Many men have lived in relationships where love felt transactional— "I'll give if you give." But real love doesn't operate on a scoreboard. Real love is generous. Real love is patient. Real love is consistent. Real love is not measured by what it gets back, but by the heart from which it is given. First Corinthians 13:5 says that love "keeps no record of wrongs," not because love ignores reality, but because love chooses connection over control.

This shift also affects how a man shows up emotionally. A man who once hid behind strength begins to show up with presence. He becomes more attentive. More engaged. More compassionate. He notices the needs of the people he loves—not because he's trying to fix everything, but because he's finally present enough to see them. He becomes a safe place for others because he has learned to be a safe place for himself.

Love given freely must also turn inward. So many men struggle with this. They can be kind to everyone else but harsh with themselves. They forgive others easily but hold themselves hostage to old mistakes. They encourage others but criticize themselves. But a man who has learned to receive love begins to extend that same grace inward. He speaks to himself with compassion. He honors his limits. He acknowledges his growth. He treats himself as someone God loves deeply—which he is.

And the most profound shift is this: a man who gives love freely no longer fears losing himself in the process. He no longer loves from insecurity or desperation. He no longer gives to be needed. He no longer sacrifices his identity to keep peace. He loves from a place of strength, not survival. From fullness, not emptiness. From truth, not fear.

This is the kind of love that transforms families, marriages, friendships, and communities. It is the kind of love that reflects the heart of God. It is the kind of love that flows from a healed man—a man who has learned to receive love and now knows how to give it freely.

As a man grows in his ability to give love freely, he notices that love no longer feels like a burden—it feels like a privilege. It no longer drains him; it energizes him. It no longer feels like something he has to do; it becomes something he gets to do. This shift happens because love is no longer flowing from emptiness or insecurity. It is flowing from a heart that has been filled, healed, and strengthened.

Contemporary life gives us countless examples of this shift. Think of the father who used to come home exhausted, offering only silence and distance. Now, he sits with his children, asks about their day, and listens with genuine interest. Or the husband who once avoided emotional conversations because they felt overwhelming. Now, he leans in, even when it's uncomfortable, because he understands that love requires connection, not avoidance. Or the friend who once kept everything surface-level. Now, he checks in, follows up, and shows up—not out of obligation, but out of genuine care.

Free love is also fearless love. Many men have loved cautiously, always holding something back. They feared being taken advantage of. They feared being misunderstood. They feared being hurt. But as healing takes root, fear loses its grip. A man begins to love with courage—not recklessness, but courage. He understands that love is always a risk, but it is a risk worth taking. First John 4:18 says, "*Perfect love drives out fear*," reminding us that love and fear cannot occupy the same space.

Consistency is another mark of love given freely. Not just on good days. Not just when he feels strong. Not just when everything is going well. But even on the days when he feels tired, uncertain, or stretched thin. Love becomes a steady rhythm, not an occasional act. This consistency builds trust. It creates safety. It deepens connection. Proverbs 3:3 says, "*Let love and faithfulness never leave you,*" reminding us that love is most powerful when it is steady.

This shift also affects how a man handles the imperfections of others. A man who has learned to give love freely becomes more patient. He becomes more understanding. He becomes more gracious. He no longer expects perfection from the people he loves because he no longer expects perfection from himself. He understands that love is not about fixing people—it is about walking with them. It is about offering grace where he once offered judgment. It is about choosing connection over criticism.

Perhaps the most Christlike expression of free love is loving people who cannot give anything back. It shows up in kindness to strangers. In compassion for the hurting. In generosity toward those in need. In forgiveness toward those who have wounded him. Jesus said in Luke 6:35, "Love your enemies… and you will be children of the Most High," reminding us that love is most powerful when it is given without expectation.

And the most profound shift is this: a man who gives love freely becomes a man who reflects the heart of God. His love becomes a testimony. His presence becomes a blessing. His words become healing. His actions become ministry. He becomes a conduit of the same love that healed him.

Giving love freely is not about perfection, it is about authenticity. It is about showing up with a whole heart. It is about loving from a place of strength, not survival. It is about offering to others what God has so graciously offered to you.

And the man who learns to give love freely becomes a man who changes the atmosphere everywhere he goes.

Loving people where they are—not where we wish they were—is one of the most challenging aspects of free love. It requires patience. It requires humility. It requires grace. It requires seeing people through God's eyes rather than through the lens of our expectations. Romans 15:7 says, "*Accept one another… just as Christ accepted you,*" reminding us that love is not about fixing people—it is about embracing them.

This kind of love transforms relationships. A spouse feels safer. Children feel more secure. Friends feel more valued. Even strangers feel seen. Love becomes a presence that others can feel, even without words. It becomes a steady, calming force in a world filled with anxiety and noise.

Free love is also wise love. It does not mean tolerating abuse, enabling dysfunction, or sacrificing your identity. It means loving with boundaries. Loving with clarity. Loving with discernment. Loving with strength. Jesus loved freely, but He also walked away from crowds, confronted hypocrisy, and protected His purpose. Healthy love is not blind—it is balanced.

Giving love freely is not the end of a man's healing—it is the evidence of it.

This presence shows up in simple ways. A man who once rushed through conversations now slows down and listens. A man who once avoided emotional moments now leans into them. A man who once kept his heart guarded now shares it with wisdom and courage. A man who once feared vulnerability now understands that vulnerability is the birthplace of connection. His love becomes a shelter, not a shield.

Free love expresses itself through service—not service rooted in obligation, but service rooted in compassion. He helps because he wants to, not because he feels pressured to. He supports others because he sees their humanity, not because he needs to prove his own. Jesus said in Mark 10:45 that He came "not to be served, but to serve," and a healed man begins to embody that same spirit—serving with humility, generosity, and joy.

This kind of love leaves a mark on families, marriages, friendships, and communities. It creates generational change. It breaks cycles of silence, anger, and emotional distance. It teaches sons how to love. It teaches daughters what love should look like. It strengthens marriages. It deepens friendships. It builds trust. It restores hope.

Giving love freely is not the end of a man's journey—it is the beginning of a new one. A journey where love is no longer something he fears, questions, or withholds. It is something he embodies. Something he expresses. Something he lives.

• • •

REFLECT

1. Are you giving love from overflow or from obligation? How can you tell the difference?
2. Who in your life needs to hear words of affirmation from you this week?
3. What does it look like to love yourself with the same grace God extends to you?

CHAPTER 14

Becoming a Whole Man

There comes a moment in a man's healing journey when he realizes that wholeness is not about having everything figured out — it is about living with nothing hidden. It is about becoming the same man privately that he is publicly. It is about living with integrity, emotional honesty, spiritual grounding, and relational depth. Wholeness is not perfection; it is alignment. It is the heart, mind, soul, and body moving in the same direction.

For years, many men have lived fragmented lives. One part of them is strong and dependable. Another part is wounded and silent. One part is confidence. Another part is afraid. One part is spiritual. Another part is numb. These pieces rarely speak to each other. They coexist, but they do not connect. And because of that, a man may function well on the outside while feeling lost on the inside.

I lived that fragmentation for longer than I like to admit. And what I want to tell you — before we go any further — is what that fragmentation actually looked like from the inside, because I think naming it honestly is more useful to you than describing it in the abstract.

WHAT FRAGMENTATION LOOKED LIKE FOR ME

There was a version of me that showed up for people with encouragement, presence, and steady faith. That man was real. I am not saying I was performing something I didn't believe. But there was another version of me — quieter, more private, known to very few — who carried wounds I hadn't processed, regrets I hadn't surrendered, and a loneliness I masked so well that most people who loved me had no idea it was there.

I was fragmented in the way many men are fragmented: not dramatically, not obviously, but in the daily gap between who I presented to the world and who I actually was when no one was watching. The minister and the man. The father who showed up and the father who carried guilt for the ways he hadn't. The one who spoke about God's grace and the one who quietly wondered whether that grace fully extended to everything he had done and left undone.

That gap — between the public man and the private one — is exhausting to maintain. And I regret the years I spent maintaining it, not because the public man was dishonest exactly, but because the private man deserved to be known too. He deserved to be brought into the light. He deserved the same grace I was telling other people to receive.

What I most regret about my fragmented years is not any single mistake. It is the accumulated cost of living divided. The relationships that couldn't go as deep as they could have because I was managing what people saw. The prayers that stayed on the surface because I was protecting even God from the full picture. The opportunities to be truly known that I let pass because I wasn't sure what would happen if someone saw them all the way through.

Wholeness begins when a man stops running from the parts of himself, he doesn't understand. It begins when he stops hiding the parts he thinks are unlovable. It begins when he stops pretending that the pain didn't affect him. It begins when he stops performing and starts living honestly. Psalm 86:11

says, "*Give me an undivided heart*," and that is the cry of a man who is ready to become whole.

THE BEGINNING OF WHOLENESS

One of the first steps toward wholeness is acknowledging the truth about your story. Not the edited version. Not the version you tell to keep people comfortable. The real version — the one that includes the wounds, the losses, the regrets, the mistakes, the victories, and the grace that carried you through.

For me, becoming whole meant acknowledging the grief I carried from losing Brittany and losing my brother Manuel. It meant admitting that those losses shaped me more than I wanted to admit — that I had moved past them in public while still carrying them privately. It meant recognizing that my silence was not strength. It was survival. And survival, as I have said before, is not the same as living.

It also meant something more personal and more difficult. It meant sitting with the honest reality of the man I had been in my marriage — the ways I had been emotionally unavailable, the ways silence had created distance where closeness should have been, the ways I had prioritized appearing capable over actually being present. It meant acknowledging that the divorce was not something that simply happened to me. I was a participant in the fracturing, and owning that — not with self-destruction, but with honest accountability — was one of the most important things I ever did.

I did not arrive at that acknowledgment easily or quickly. It came in layers, over time, as God patiently worked on the parts of me, I had kept locked. But when I finally got there, something shifted. Not all at once. But steadily, the way a room fills with light when you open the curtains one window at a time.

Wholeness also requires embracing the parts of yourself you once rejected. The emotional part. The tender part. The vulnerable part. The part that feels deeply. The part that needs connection. The part that longs for love. Many men were taught to suppress these parts because they were labeled weak. But these parts are not weaknesses — they are the very places where God meets us. They are the places where healing begins.

A whole man is not a man without wounds — he is a man who has learned to integrate them. He does not deny his past; he redeems it. He does not hide his scars; he honors them. He does not pretend to be invincible; he embraces his humanity. This kind of honesty creates freedom. It creates peace. It creates a life where a man no longer has to perform — he can simply be.

WHAT WHOLENESS PRODUCED

I want to tell you what changed when wholeness began to take root in me, because I think testimony is more convincing than theory.

When I remarried and Shannon became my wife, I brought a different man to that marriage than the one I had been before. Not a perfect man — I want to be clear about that. But an honest one. A man who had sat with his failures long enough to understand them. A man who had learned, through hard and humbling experience, what emotional absence costs the people you love. A man who was no longer willing to keep the gap between his public self and his private one.

I loved Shannon differently than I had loved before. Not because I tried harder, but because God had done something in me through the breaking and the healing that made me capable of a depth of love and honesty I simply had not possessed before. The losses, the regrets, the slow work of becoming whole — all of it prepared me to be a husband and a father in ways that striving alone never could have.

And when God added three more children to my life through that marriage — two sons and another daughter — I understood something about redemption that I could not have understood any other way. God does not just restore what was broken. He multiplies it. He adds to it. He exceeds what you thought you had lost and gives you more than you knew how to ask for. That is not something I take lightly. That is the faithfulness of God made personal and specific and undeniable.

I am grateful — not for the pain, exactly, but for what God produced through it. I am grateful that He did not leave me in my fragmentation. I am grateful that He was patient enough to work on me in layers, on His timetable, without rushing what needed time to heal. I am grateful that the man I am today — imperfect still, still growing, still learning — is more honest, more present, more genuinely loving than the man I was when I thought I had it all together.

That is wholeness. Not arrival. Not perfection. But genuine, integrated, ongoing transformation.

WHAT WHOLENESS LOOKS LIKE EVERY DAY

When wholeness began in me, I saw it most clearly in my relationships. I started to show up with consistency, reliability, and true presence. I no longer checked out emotionally when things got hard, nor did I run from tough conversations or hide behind a mask of silence or strength. Instead, I chose to lean in — to communicate honestly, to apologize when I was wrong, to forgive quickly, and to listen deeply. As I became healthier, my relationships grew healthier too. Wholeness didn't just change how I felt inside — it changed how I connected with the people I love.

Wholeness also affects how a man sees himself. A man who once defined himself by his mistakes now sees himself through the lens of grace. A man who once carried shame now walks in forgiveness. A man who once felt unworthy now understands his value. Second Corinthians 5:17 says, "If anyone is in Christ, he is a new creation." Wholeness is the lived expression of that truth — not as a theological statement, but as a daily reality.

Wholeness also brings spiritual depth. A man who once approached God out of duty now approaches Him out of desire. His prayers become more honest. His worship becomes more heartfelt. His faith becomes more personal. He no longer hides his wounds from God — he brings them into the light. He no longer tries to earn God's approval — he rests in God's love.

Wholeness also affects how a man handles temptation — not just moral temptation, but emotional temptation. The temptation to shut down. The temptation to isolate. The temptation to pretend. The temptation to revert to old patterns. A whole man recognizes these temptations for what they are: invitations to return to a version of himself he has outgrown. Instead of giving in, he chooses truth. He chooses growth. He chooses the man he is becoming.

Wholeness also shows up in how a man relates to others. A whole man loves without fear, listens without defensiveness, apologizes without shame, and forgives without resentment. He is not perfect, but he is present. He is not flawless, but he is grounded. He is not without struggle, but he is no longer ruled by it. His relationships become healthier because he is healthier. His presence becomes safer because he is no longer hiding.

And perhaps the most powerful truth is this: wholeness is not something you achieve alone. It is something God builds in you — by His healing, His love, His truth, the community He surrounds you with, and His grace at every step. The work He began in you; He intends to finish. Wholeness is His work. You simply cooperate with it.

This mean wholeness is not a destination — it is a way of living. It is the daily choice to show up as your true self. It is the courage to live with nothing hidden. It is the freedom to be fully human and fully loved. It is not about never being broken again — it is about knowing what to do when life breaks you. A whole man does not avoid pain; he processes it. He does not deny struggle; he works through it. He does not pretend to be invincible; he embraces his humanity with grace.

And the man who becomes whole becomes a man who can finally live fully — not despite everything he has been through, but because of what God did with it.

That is the promise I am standing on.

And it is the same promise He is holding out to you.

• • •

REFLECT

1. Describe the gap between your public self and your private self. What would it cost you to close it? What might it give you?

2. What parts of yourself have you been hiding because you thought they were unlovable — and what might God want to do with those very parts?
3. What would wholeness look like in your most important relationship if you showed up as the same man privately that you are publicly?

CHAPTER 15

Walking in Your God-Given Purpose

Walking in Your God-Given Purpose. There comes a moment in a man's healing journey when he realizes that wholeness is not the finish line—it is the foundation. Healing prepares a man for something greater. It prepares him to live with intention, clarity, and spiritual authority. It prepares him to step into the purpose God designed for him long before he took his first breath. Purpose is not something a man creates; it is something he uncovers. It is something he grows into. It is something he walks out.

For years, many men have lived in survival mode. They worked, provided, endured, and pushed through because life demanded it. Purpose was a luxury they didn't have time to consider. They were too busy trying to stay afloat. But once a man becomes whole—once he stops running from himself, once he stops hiding behind strength, once he stops living fragmented—he becomes ready to hear God's voice in a new way. He becomes ready to ask the question he avoided for years: "Why am I here?"

Purpose is not about titles, positions, or accomplishments. It is not about being impressive. It is not about being successful in the eyes of others. Purpose is about alignment—aligning your gifts, your story, your passion, and your faith with the assignment God has placed on your life. Ephesians 2:10 says, "*We are His workmanship, created in Christ Jesus for good works, which God prepared beforehand.*" That means your purpose is older than your pain. Older than your mistakes. Older than your fears. Older than your doubts. God wrote your purpose before life tried to rewrite your identity.

For me, walking in purpose meant acknowledging that the losses I endured—losing Brittany, losing Manuel—were not just tragedies; they were turning points. They awakened something in me. They deepened my compassion. They sharpened my voice. They clarified my calling. They taught me how to walk with men who are grieving, struggling, or silently breaking. My purpose was not born from my strength—it was born from my wounds. And God used those wounds to shape the man I am becoming.

Purpose also requires listening. Not to the noise of expectations. Not to the pressure of culture. Not to the opinions of people who don't know your story. Purpose requires listening to the quiet, steady voice of God. The voice that speaks in prayer. The voice that whispers in stillness. The voice that nudges you toward something bigger than yourself. Psalm 32:8 says, "*I will instruct you and teach you in the way you should go.*" Purpose is not discovered through striving—it is revealed through relationship.

Another step in walking in purpose is embracing your gifts. Many men downplay their gifts because they don't see them as special. They think, "Anyone can do this." But that is not true. Your gifts are fingerprints of God's intention. Your ability to encourage, to lead, to create, to teach, to build, to comfort, to inspire—these are not accidents. They are clues. They are indicators. They are signposts pointing toward your calling.

Purpose also requires courage. Walking in purpose means stepping into places that feel unfamiliar. It means doing things you've never done. It means trusting God more than your comfort zone. It means believing that you are equipped, even when you feel inadequate. Moses didn't feel ready. Gideon didn't feel qualified. Jeremiah didn't feel capable. But God doesn't call the qualified—He qualifies the called.

And perhaps the most important truth is this: purpose is not something you chase—it is something you become. It is the natural expression of a healed, whole, grounded man who is aligned with God. It flows from identity. It flows from wholeness. It flows from love. It flows from truth.

Purpose is not a destination—it is a way of living.

As a man begins to walk in his God-given purpose, he discovers that purpose is not a single moment of revelation—it is a series of decisions, steps, and alignments. Purpose unfolds gradually, like a sunrise. It doesn't rush. It doesn't overwhelm. It reveals itself one layer at a time, one season at a time, one act of obedience at a time. And as it unfolds, a man begins to see that purpose is not something he performs—it is something he lives.

Another sign is alignment. A man walking in purpose begins to feel a deep internal "yes" when he is moving in the direction God designed for him. His gifts feel natural. His passion feels alive. His spirit feels settled. His decisions feel intentional. He no longer forces himself into roles that drain him or relationships that diminish him. He no longer tries to be who others expect him to be. He becomes aligned with who God created him to be.

Walking in purpose also means embracing responsibility. Purpose is not passive. It requires discipline. It requires commitment. It requires stewardship. It requires showing up even when you don't feel like it. It requires faithfulness in the small things. Luke 16:10 says, "Whoever is faithful with little will be faithful with much." Purpose grows in the soil of consistency.

Purpose is something a man grows into every day.

As a man grows into his God-given purpose, he begins to realize that purpose is not something he visits—it is something he inhabits. It becomes part of his identity, part of his rhythm, part of his daily walk. Purpose stops being a question he asks and becomes a truth he lives. And as he lives it, he discovers that purpose is less about what he does and more about who he becomes.

This confidence shows up in everyday moments. Think of the man who once hesitated to speak because he feared being misunderstood. Now, he speaks with clarity because he knows his voice matters. Or the man who once avoided leadership because he doubted his ability. Now, he steps forward because he understands that leadership is not about perfection, it is about service. Or the man who once hid his gifts because he didn't want to stand out. Now, he uses them boldly because he knows they were given to him for a reason.

Purpose also brings clarity about relationships. A man walking in purpose becomes more discerning about who he allows into his life. He recognizes that not everyone can walk with him into the next season. Some relationships were for survival. Some were for comfort. Some were for a chapter, not the whole story. Purpose requires alignment, and alignment requires discernment. Amos 3:3 asks, "Can two walk together unless they agree?" A man walking in purpose chooses relationships that support his calling, not sabotage it.

This discernment is not harsh—it is healthy. It allows a man to love people without losing himself. It allows him to set boundaries without guilt. It allows him to walk away from what drains him and walk toward what grows him. It allows him to invest in relationships that are mutual, life-giving, and aligned with God's direction.

Purpose also brings spiritual authority. A man walking in purpose prays differently. He worships differently. He listens differently. He obeys differently. He no longer approaches God as someone who is lost—he approaches God as someone who is led. He no longer prays from fear, he prays from faith. He no longer asks, "Lord, are You with me?" He begins to declare, "*Lord, I am with You.*" John 15:16 says, "You did not choose Me, but I chose you and appointed you," and a man walking in purpose begins to live like he believes that.

This spiritual authority is not loud—it is steady. It is not showy, it is rooted. It is not about being impressive, it is about being obedient. It is the authority of a man who knows he is walking in the assignment God gave him.

Purpose is not something a man discovers once—it is something he grows into every day.

As a man steps fully into his God-given purpose, he begins to understand that purpose is not about being impressive—it is about being faithful. It is not about being seen—it is about being sent. It is not about building a platform—it is about building people. Purpose is not measured by applause, visibility, or recognition. It is measured by obedience. It is measured by impact. It is measured by the quiet, consistent "yes" a man gives to God day after day.

Purpose shows up in the simplest moments of a man's day. The man who once kept his story to himself now shares it with someone who needs hope. The man who once doubted his voice now speaks with clarity and compassion. The man who once felt unqualified now mentors younger men because he knows his journey has value. Purpose turns ordinary moments into ministry.

This legacy is built in quiet moments. In the way he loves. In the way he forgives. In the way he shows up. In the way he prays. In the way he leads. In the way he treats people. In the way he carries himself. Legacy is not something he announces, it is something he lives.

And the man who walks in purpose becomes a man who changes the world around him—one step, one act of obedience, one life at a time.

• • •

REFLECT

1. What gifts, experiences, or passions has God given you that point toward your purpose?
2. What pain in your life might God be transforming into your calling?
3. What is one step of obedience God is asking you to take right now?

CHAPTER 16

Living With Emotional and Spiritual Authority

There comes a moment in a man's journey when he realizes that healing was never meant to weaken him. It was meant to make him steady. Not the kind of strength that hides pain or pretends to be unshakable, but the kind that grows from being rooted, honest, and spiritually anchored. This is the quiet strength of a man who has learned to live with emotional and spiritual authority.

Authority is not loud or forceful. It doesn't need to dominate a room or prove anything. True authority feels like calm clarity. It is the ability to stand in who you are without being pushed around by fear, insecurity, or the expectations of others. It shows up in the way a man speaks truth gently, loves without hesitation, and walks in purpose without apology.

Many men struggle with authority because they struggle with identity. They appear strong on the outside but feel uncertain on the inside. They show up for everyone else but feel disconnected from themselves. They know God yet carry emotional wounds that keep them fragmented. But when a man begins to heal — when he learns to receive love, offer love, and live with intention — authority rises in him naturally. It is not something he performs; it is something he grows into.

Another sign is emotional steadiness. A man who once reacted out of old wounds begins to respond from a healthier place. He becomes more consistent, more grounded, more trustworthy. His presence brings calm instead of tension. His words bring clarity instead of confusion. His choices reflect who he is becoming, not what he is afraid of.

Authority also shapes how a man handles conflict. He doesn't run from it, and he doesn't inflame it. He listens. He seeks understanding. He values connection more than being right. He chooses peace without abandoning truth. This kind of presence strengthens relationships because it creates safety and respect.

Spiritual authority grows alongside emotional maturity. A man with spiritual authority knows who he is in God — loved, forgiven, chosen, and called. He understands that he carries God's presence into every space he enters. He believes his prayers matter. He trusts that his obedience has weight. Luke 10:19 speaks of this authority, and when a man embraces it, he walks with a different posture.

Spiritual authority is not about being religious; it is about being aligned. It is living in step with God — listening, trusting, and obeying. It is humility, integrity, and courage woven together. It is living in such a way that heaven recognizes your voice and darkness recognizes your strength.

A man with authority also protects his peace. He becomes careful with what he allows into his mind and spirit. He sets boundaries not out of fear, but out of wisdom. He guards his heart because he understands its value.

In the end, emotional and spiritual authority are not about controlling others. They are about becoming whole — living from a place of identity, purpose, and quiet strength. They are about becoming the man God intended: grounded, compassionate, wise, and anchored.

There comes a time in a man's healing when he realizes that strength is not found in how much he carries, but in how deeply he is rooted. Life will always bring responsibilities, pressures, and moments that stretch him, but a man who has learned to live from his center moves through those moments differently. He is no longer driven by fear or shaped by old wounds. He begins to live from a place of quiet stability — a place where his soul is anchored and his spirit is settled.

Living from your center is not about perfection. It is about alignment. It is about learning to return to the place within you where God speaks, where peace lives, and where clarity rises. Every man has a center, but not every man knows how to live from it. Many men live from their reactions, their insecurities, their past, or their pressure to perform. But a man who has done the inner work learns to live from a deeper place — a place where truth guides him more than emotion, and purpose steadies him more than fear.

Living from your center also changes the way you respond to life. A man who once reacted quickly now responds thoughtfully. He no longer lets anger speak for him. He no longer lets fear silence him. He no longer lets insecurity drive him. He becomes steady — not because life is easier, but because he is anchored. His responses come from a place of clarity rather than chaos. His decisions come from conviction rather than pressure. His words come from truth rather than emotion.

A centered man becomes a safe man. People feel at ease around him because his presence is calm, not chaotic. His tone is gentle, not sharp. His posture is open, not defensive. He carries himself with humility, not arrogance. He listens more than he speaks, and when he does speak, his words carry weight because they come from a place of sincerity. This kind of presence is not learned overnight — it is formed through healing, reflection, and a willingness to grow.

Spiritually, living from your center means living in step with God. It means allowing His voice to shape your identity, His wisdom to guide your decisions, and His presence to steady your heart. A man who lives from his center does not rush ahead of God, nor does he lag behind. He walks with Him. He trusts Him. He leans into Him. He understands that strength is not found in striving, but in surrender. Isaiah 30:15 says, "*...in quietness and trust is your strength.*" A centered man knows this to be true.

Living from your center also means living with integrity. A man who is centered does not live a divided life. He is the same man in private that he is in public. He does not compromise his values to gain approval. He does not shrink himself to avoid conflict. He does not pretend to be someone he is not. Integrity becomes his anchor, and authenticity becomes his language. He understands that the greatest freedom is being fully himself — the man God created him to be.

And perhaps the most beautiful part of living from your center is the way it transforms your relationships. A centered man loves differently. He loves with patience, not pressure. He loves with presence, not performance. He loves with honesty, not fear. His relationships become healthier because he is healthier. His connections become deeper because he is deeper. His love becomes safer because he is safe.

Living from your center is not a destination — it is a daily practice. It is choosing, again and again, to return to the place where your soul is grounded, your spirit is steady, and your identity is secure. It is choosing to live from the inside out rather than the outside in. It is choosing to be the man God intended — whole, rooted, peaceful, and aligned.

This is the gift of healing. This is the fruit of growth. This is the life of a man who has learned to live from his center.

Every man loses his center from time to time. Life has a way of pulling at the soul — responsibilities stack up, emotions get stirred, old wounds resurface, and the noise of the world grows louder than the voice within. Losing your center does not mean you have failed. It simply means you are human. What matters is learning how to return to the place where your heart is steady and your spirit is aligned.

A man begins to find his center when he learns to slow down. Not just physically, but internally. He gives himself permission to pause, to breathe, to step back from the rush and reconnect with what is happening inside him. Stillness becomes a doorway. In the quiet, he can hear what he has been avoiding. He can feel what he has been carrying. He can sense what needs attention. Psalm 46:10 whispers, "*Be still, and know that I am God.*" Stillness is not inactivity — it is intentional presence.

Another way a man returns to his center is through honesty. Not the kind of honesty that is harsh or self-critical, but the kind that is gentle and truthful. He admits when he is overwhelmed. He acknowledges when he is drifting. He recognizes when he is operating from fear instead of faith. This kind of honesty is not weakness — it is clarity. It allows him to see where he is so he can move toward where he needs to be.

A man also finds his center through connection. Healing is not meant to be done alone. Sometimes God uses the presence of others to steady us — a trusted friend, a wise mentor, a loving partner, or a spiritual brother who knows how to listen without judgment. When a man allows himself to be supported, he discovers that strength is not found in isolation but in community.

Returning to your center also requires boundaries. A man cannot stay centered if he is constantly pulled in every direction. He learns to say "no" when necessary. He learns to step away from environments that drain him. He learns to protect his peace the way a gardener protects the soil — not out of fear, but out of wisdom. Boundaries are not walls; they are gates. They allow in what nourishes and keep out what harms.

A man finds his center through prayer. Not just formal prayer, but the simple, honest conversations with God that happen throughout the day. Prayer recenters the heart. It reminds a man who he is and whose he is. It shifts his focus from pressure to presence, from striving to surrender. Prayer is not about getting everything right — it is about staying connected to the One who holds everything together.

A man also returns to his center by remembering what is true. When life becomes loud, lies become tempting — lies about his worth, his identity, his future, and his strength. But truth has a way of grounding the soul. Truth reminds him that he is loved, chosen, forgiven, and called. Truth reminds him that he is not alone. Truth reminds him that God is with him, for him, and working through him. When a man anchors himself in truth, fear loses its grip.

And finally, a man finds his center by practicing grace. He gives himself permission to grow slowly. He allows himself to be imperfect. He understands that healing is not linear and growth is not instant. Grace softens the pressure he puts on himself. Grace allows him to begin again. Grace reminds him that God is patient, and he can be patient with himself too.

Living from your center is not about never losing it — it is about knowing how to return. It is about recognizing the signs, slowing down, reconnecting with God, and choosing alignment over anxiety. It is about living from the inside out, not the outside in. It is about becoming the man God intended — grounded, peaceful, steady, and whole.

When a man learns to live from his center, the change within him does not stay contained. It begins to shape the world around him in quiet, powerful ways. A centered man carries something different — not because he tries to, but because alignment naturally produces influence. His presence becomes a steady force. His words carry weight. His life becomes a reflection of the work God has done in him.

A centered man influences others first through his presence. He doesn't have to be the loudest voice in the room or the most charismatic personality. His strength is not in performance; it is in peace. People feel safer around him because he is not unpredictable. He is not ruled by emotion or ego. He is grounded. His calm becomes contagious. His steadiness becomes shelter. His presence communicates, "You don't have to be afraid here."

A centered man also influences through the way he listens. He listens without rushing to fix. He listens without judgment. He listens with compassion, not impatience. In a world where many people feel unheard, a man who listens well becomes a gift. His listening creates space for others to breathe, to open up, to be honest. It builds trust. It strengthens connection. It communicates value without needing to say a word.

His leadership changes too. A centered man leads from humility, not insecurity. He leads from clarity, not pressure. He leads from purpose, not pride. He does not need to control people to feel powerful. He does not need to dominate to feel respected. His leadership is steady, thoughtful, and rooted in integrity. People follow him not because they fear him, but because they trust him. Proverbs 11:3 says, "*The integrity of the upright guides them.*" Integrity becomes his compass, and others feel safe following a man who is guided by truth.

Spiritually, a centered man carries a different weight. He walks with a sense of God's presence that others can feel. His prayers are not loud, but they are sincere. His faith is not performative, but it is steady. He trusts God in a way that inspires others to trust Him too. He becomes a living reminder that spiritual authority is not about position — it is about alignment. When a man is aligned with God, his life becomes a reflection of heaven's order.

But the deepest influence of a centered man may be the simplest: he gives others permission to heal. His life becomes an invitation. His growth becomes a roadmap. His steadiness becomes a testimony that healing is possible, wholeness is real, and God truly restores what was broken.

• • •

REFLECT

1. Where do you need to grow in emotional authority—naming your feelings without being ruled by them?
2. What does spiritual authority look like in your daily life, not just in church?
3. How can you protect your peace this week without withdrawing from people who need you?

CHAPTER 17

Learning to Live from Rest

There comes a moment in a man's journey when he realizes that rest is not optional — it is essential. It is not weakness — it is wisdom. It is not laziness — it is alignment. Rest is not simply the absence of activity; it is the presence of peace. It is the ability to live without being driven by fear, pressure, or the need to prove something. Rest is the posture of a man who knows who he is, where he stands, and who holds his life.

Many men have lived most of their lives without rest. They were taught to grind, push, endure, and keep going no matter what. They learned to measure their worth by productivity, performance, and how much they could carry. They believed that slowing down meant falling behind. They believed that rest was something you earned, not something you needed. But emotional and spiritual maturity reveal a deeper truth: rest is part of God's design for a man's strength.

I didn't realize how long I had been living on emotional fumes. Men are good at that — running on empty, convincing ourselves that "I'm fine" is a strategy instead of a warning sign. I had become so accustomed to pushing through that I didn't even recognize the weight I was carrying anymore. It wasn't one big thing; it was the accumulation of a thousand small pressures, disappointments, expectations, and unspoken fears that had settled into my soul like dust. And dust, if you don't deal with it, eventually becomes a layer thick enough to change the color of everything.

There were days when I felt like I was performing my life instead of living it. Smiling when I was tired. Encouraging others when I was empty. Showing up strong when I felt fragile. I wasn't lying — I was surviving. But survival has a way of numbing you. It teaches you to function without feeling, to move without meaning, to exist without truly being present. And the danger is that people will applaud your strength while having no idea you're slowly fading behind your own eyes.

I remember one evening sitting alone in my car after a long day. I didn't turn on the radio. I didn't reach for my phone. I just sat there, staring at the steering wheel, feeling the weight of everything I had been pretending didn't bother me. It wasn't a breakdown. It wasn't a crisis. It was a quiet moment of truth — the kind that sneaks up on you when the noise finally stops. I whispered, almost without thinking, "Lord… I'm tired." Not physically. Not even mentally. I was tired in a place deeper than language.

And in that stillness, I sensed something I hadn't felt in a long time: God wasn't disappointed in me. He wasn't shaking His head, telling me to toughen up. He wasn't reminding me of all the people who needed me. He was simply present. Gentle. Patient. Almost as if He had been waiting for me to finally stop pretending I was okay.

Men often believe that admitting exhaustion is the same as admitting defeat. But exhaustion is not failure — it's information. It's your soul saying, "Something needs to change." It's God whispering, "You were never meant to carry this alone." Jesus didn't say, "Come to Me, all you who are strong enough to keep going." He said, "Come to Me, all you who are weary and burdened, and I will give you rest." Rest is not a reward for finishing the race. Rest is part of the race.

That night in the car, I realized I had been living as if God expected me to be invincible. But the truth is, He never asked me to be a superhero. He asked me to be His son. And sons don't earn rest — they receive it.

Something shifted in me that evening. Not dramatically. Not instantly. But enough for me to recognize that I had been carrying responsibilities God never assigned to me. I had been trying to fix things I didn't break, hold things I couldn't control, and sustain things I didn't have the strength to maintain. And the more I tried to hold it all together, the more I was falling apart on the inside.

Letting go didn't mean quitting. It meant surrendering. It meant acknowledging that I am human — beautifully, intentionally, purposefully human — and that God is God. It meant giving myself permission to breathe again, to feel again, to rest again. It meant trusting that the world would not collapse if I stopped trying to hold it up.

As I began to face the truth of my own exhaustion, something unexpected happened: the world around me didn't fall apart. The responsibilities I had been gripping so tightly didn't suddenly collapse. Life kept moving, people kept living, and God kept being God. It was humbling to realize that the weight I thought I was holding up was never resting on my shoulders in the first place. I had confused stewardship with ownership, duty with identity, and strength with silence.

One of the hardest truths I had to face was this: I had been living as if God needed me. As if the people I loved would crumble without my constant strength. As if the ministry would fall apart if I didn't hold every piece together. But God never asked me to be the source — only a vessel. And vessels don't produce anything; they simply carry what's been poured into them.

When a vessel is empty, it doesn't need to try harder. It needs to be filled.

That realization forced me to confront another truth: I had been pouring out far more than I had been receiving. I was giving encouragement without receiving any. I was offering wisdom without sitting still long enough to hear God's. I was showing up for others while quietly disappearing from myself. So, I began to do something that felt foreign at first: I started telling the truth.

Not the polished truth. Not the "I'm blessed and highly favored" truth. The real truth — the truth that said, "I'm struggling today." And instead of losing respect, I gained connection. Instead of being seen as weak, I was seen as human. And instead of feeling alone, I felt understood.

There is a sacred strength in honesty. It doesn't diminish a man — it frees him. It frees him from the pressure to perform, the fear of disappointing others, and the lie that vulnerability is a liability. It frees him to be loved, not for what he does, but for who he is. And that kind of love is the only love that heals.

I began to see that God wasn't just healing my exhaustion; He was healing the beliefs that created it. He was confronting the lies I had carried for years — lies that sounded noble but were quietly destroying me. Lies like:

"If I don't do it, it won't get done."

"If I show weakness, people will lose confidence in me."

"If I rest, I'm being irresponsible."

"If I slow down, I'll fall behind."

"If I don't hold everything together, everything will fall apart."

These lies had shaped my behavior, my relationships, my decisions, and even my prayers. They had convinced me that God's love was tied to my performance and that my worth was tied to my usefulness. But the truth is, God loved me before I ever accomplished anything. And He wasn't impressed by my strength — He was drawn to my honesty.

As I let go of those lies, I started to experience a different kind of strength — a strength rooted not in effort, but in surrender. A strength that didn't come from pushing harder, but from trusting deeper. A strength that didn't require me to be invincible but invited me to be authentic.

And authenticity changed everything.

It changed the way I prayed. My prayers became less about asking God to help me carry more and more about asking Him to show me what I was never meant to carry in the first place.

It changed the way I loved. I stopped loving from a place of depletion and started loving from a place of overflow.

It changed the way I saw myself. I stopped seeing myself as a machine and started seeing myself as a man — a man with limits, needs, emotions, and a soul that deserved care.

WHAT REST PRODUCES

Living from rest doesn't mean withdrawing from life — it means moving through it differently. A man who has learned to rest is not easily shaken. He is not reactive. He is not overwhelmed by every shift in circumstance. He moves with intention, speaks with clarity and responds with wisdom. He has come to know that he draws his strength from stillness rather than striving.

Rest also calls a man to slow his internal pace, not just his external one. Many men reduce their activity but never quiet their minds. They stop moving, but they don't stop worrying. Rest requires internal stillness — the ability to quiet the noise, silence the pressure, and breathe deeply. Psalm 46:10 says, "*Be still, and know that I am God,*" and a man who lives from rest learns to let stillness become a spiritual practice.

This shows up in how he relates to others. He no longer enters relationships from a place of depletion. He no longer gives what he does not have. Instead, he loves from overflow, not obligation. He gives from fullness, not emptiness. He shows up with presence, not exhaustion. Rest makes him a better partner, father, friend, and leader.

A man grounded in rest also embraces rhythms — daily, weekly, and seasonal rhythms that keep him aligned. Jesus Himself modeled this: withdrawing to pray, resting with His disciples, honoring the Sabbath, moving with intention rather than urgency. A rested man follows this pattern. He creates space for renewal. He honors his limits. He understands that rest is not a reward — it is a requirement.

Rest teaches a man to detach from unnecessary battles. He no longer fights every fight. He no longer argues to be right. He chooses his battles with wisdom. He understands that not every conflict deserves his energy. Rest gives him discernment — discernment to walk away, to stay silent, or to stand firm. And it gives him patience — patience with himself, patience with others, and patience with the journey.

A man who lives from rest also shapes his relationship with God. He no longer approaches God only when he is desperate or depleted. He approaches Him daily, consistently, quietly. He listens more and strives less. He prays from a place of connection, instead of crisis. Rest becomes the steady ground he walks on, the place where God quiets him, restores him, and renews his soul day after day.

Rest is not something a man finds — it is something he chooses. It is the decision to trust God more than his own effort. It is the decision to release what he cannot control. It is the decision to live from peace rather than pressure.

And slowly, rest is not something he visits — it is who he becomes.

And slowly, I realized something profound: rest is not the absence of responsibility; it is the presence of God. When a man learns to rest in God, he doesn't become weaker — he becomes wiser. He becomes clearer. He becomes more grounded, more centered, more whole. He becomes the man God intended, not the man life pressured him to be.

Part of my healing was learning to breathe again — not just physically, but spiritually. To breathe without guilt. To breathe without fear. To breathe without apologizing for being human. And in that breath, I found a freedom I didn't know I needed.

Because the truth is, God never asked me to be the hero of my own story. He asked me to trust the One who already is.

• • •

REFLECT

1. What has the weight you've been carrying been costing you — emotionally, physically, spiritually?
2. What lie about rest do you most need to release today?
3. What would change if you believed that rest is not earned but designed by God for your strength?

CHAPTER 18

Walking in the New Way

There is a moment in every man's journey when the inner work begins to show up in the outer life. The emptiness that once defined him has been filled. The lies he once believed have been confronted. The burdens he was never meant to carry have been laid down. Now, something shifts. The change that has been happening inside him starts to become visible — not in dramatic ways, not in ways that draw attention, but in quiet shifts that reveal something deeper has changed.

This is where a man begins to walk in the identity Jesus has been forming within him.

For so long, many of us lived from old patterns — patterns shaped by fear, pressure, insecurity, or survival. We reacted instead of responding. We carried instead of trusting. We hid instead of healing. But when Jesus fills the empty places, those old patterns begin to lose their grip. They don't disappear overnight, but they no longer feel like home. Something inside us knows there is a better way now — a way shaped by grace, truth, and identity.

HOW JESUS RESTORES

There is a tenderness in the way Jesus restores a man that often goes unnoticed. We expect Him to come with power, with force, with dramatic transformation. But more often, He comes quietly — like morning light slipping through a window, slowly revealing what was always there but had been hidden in the dark.

Many men come to Him carrying years of silence, shame, or self-reliance. They don't know how to pray yet. They only know they're tired, empty, and longing for something real. And Jesus meets them right there — not with demands, but with welcome.

For years, I thought restoration meant God would fix my circumstances — change the people around me, open the doors I wanted, make life smoother. But Jesus wasn't trying to rearrange my world. He was trying to rebuild my heart. He was filling places I didn't even know were empty. He was healing wounds I had learned to live with. He was softening parts of me I didn't realize had grown hard. And He was doing it gently.

That's how He fills the empty places:

Not by overwhelming us,

Not by exposing us,

But by gently drawing near.

He fills the emptiness with His peace first. A peace that doesn't make sense, but settles the soul. Then He fills it with truth — truth that replaces the lies we've believed about ourselves. Then He fills it with love — love that doesn't depend on performance or perfection. And slowly, He fills it with purpose — purpose that grows as we learn to trust Him.

He restores identity by reminding us, "You are My son." He restores dignity by whispering, "You are forgiven." He restores hope by declaring, "Your story is not over." He restores strength by saying, "My grace is enough for you."

A man who once felt empty now begins to feel held. A man who once felt lost now begins to feel led. A man who once felt unworthy now begins to feel loved. These are not small shifts — they are the beginnings of a new identity forming inside him, rooted not in what he has done, but in who Jesus is.

And as this identity takes shape, a man starts to see himself through Jesus' eyes. He begins to believe that he is worth restoring. He begins to trust that he is worth loving. He begins to accept that he is worth keeping. Jesus teaches us this slowly, gently, and consistently, until the truth sinks in: You are Mine, and I am not letting you go.

This is where the empty places become sacred places. The loneliness becomes a place of communion. The fear becomes a place of courage. The shame becomes a place of grace. The emptiness becomes a place of fullness — not because the man filled himself, but because Jesus did.

THE RENEWED MIND IN DAILY LIFE

A man knows he is beginning to walk in his new identity when the way he thinks starts to change. Not because he is trying harder, but because Jesus is reshaping him from the inside out. This is where Romans 12:2 becomes more than a verse — it becomes a lived experience: "*Do not be conformed to this world but be transformed by the renewing of your mind.*" Transformation is not behavior modification. It is not a man trying to be better. It is Jesus renewing the way he sees himself, the way he sees God, and the way he sees the world.

The old self still tries to speak. It still whispers the familiar lies: "You're not enough," "You'll never change," "You're on your own," "You're the same man you've always been." But now, those lies don't land the same way. Something inside him pushes back — gently, but firmly. Something inside him says, "That's not who I am anymore."

He begins to make decisions from peace instead of panic.

He begins to speak from truth instead of insecurity.

He begins to respond from identity instead of fear.

He begins to walk with a quiet confidence that doesn't come from himself, but from the One who is shaping him.

This is not perfection. It is direction. It is a man learning to walk in step with the Spirit, one day at a time.

He starts practicing new rhythms that align with who he is becoming. Not religious performances. Not spiritual checklists. Simple, steady choices that flow from a heart being renewed. He practices responding instead of reacting — the old self reacted quickly out of fear or frustration, but the new self responds from a place of peace. He practices returning to truth — when old thoughts of shame or inadequacy rise, he brings them into the light of what Jesus has said about him. He practices receiving grace daily — when he stumbles, he doesn't condemn himself. He gets back up, keeps walking, and trusts that Jesus is not disappointed in his progress. He is committed to it.

These rhythms are small, but they are powerful. They shape the way a man lives, the way he loves, the way he works, and the way he sees himself.

TRANSFORMATION MADE VISIBLE

As the weeks and months pass, a man begins to notice the quiet contrast between his old self and his new self. It's simply the natural evidence of a heart touched by Jesus and a mind being renewed day by day.

This transformation becomes visible first in his relationships. People around him may not know the details of his journey, but they can sense the difference. They feel safer around him. They feel heard. They feel valued. They feel the steadiness of a man who is no longer living from his wounds, but from his healing.

His home becomes calmer. His friendships become deeper. His conversations become more meaningful. His presence becomes a source of peace — not because he is trying to be impressive, but because he is learning to live from the fullness Jesus has placed within him.

This is the quiet beauty of transformation: the man who once lived from emptiness now lives from overflow.

And as he walks in this new identity, he begins to understand that the work Jesus has done inside him is not just for his own sake. Jesus never restores a man only for himself. He restores him so he can carry something into the world: peace, presence, compassion, wisdom, steadiness, love. These are not tasks — they are expressions of a renewed life.

A man walking in his new identity begins to feel a quiet pull toward purpose. He senses that God is leading him somewhere — into deeper relationships, healthier patterns, meaningful work, service, influence, legacy. He begins to realize that his life is not random. His story is not wasted. His healing is not accidental. Jesus has been shaping him for something.

And this purpose doesn't come with pressure. It comes with peace. It doesn't come with striving. It comes with surrender. He doesn't have to chase it. He simply walks in it, one step at a time, trusting that the same God who renewed his mind will guide his path.

This is where a man begins to see that his past no longer disqualifies him — it equips him. His wounds no longer define him — they deepen him. His failures no longer shame him — they humble him. His healing no longer stays private — it becomes a testimony. And his identity no longer comes from the world — it comes from the One who called him.

This is the beginning of a new rhythm.

A new way of thinking.

A new way of living.

A new way of being a man.

• • •

REFLECT

1. Where have you noticed the quiet contrast between your old self and who you are becoming?
2. What empty place has God been filling that you haven't fully acknowledged yet?
3. How has your relationship with God changed as a result of your healing journey?

CHAPTER 19

Marriage, Family, and Finances

Marriage, Family, and Finances: Living Out Transformation in the Places That Matter Most. There are three areas of a man's life where his transformation becomes the most visible, the most tested, and the most meaningful: marriage, family, and finances. These are the places where the old self once showed up the strongest — in pressure, in fear, in frustration, in striving — and they are also the places where the new identity Jesus has formed in him begins to shine the brightest.

At the end of this chapter is where the man steps into the everyday realities of life and discovers that the work Jesus has done inside him is not just personal — it is practical. It touches his home. It touches his relationships. It touches his responsibilities. It touches the way he leads, the way he loves, and the way he stewards what God has entrusted to him.

This chapter is not about perfection. It is about presence. It is about learning to bring the renewed mind and restored heart into the places where life is lived most intimately.

A man's marriage is often the first place where his new identity begins to take shape in real time. Not because marriage is easy, but because marriage is honest. It reveals the parts of us we hide from the world. It exposes the places where we still need grace. It invites us to love in ways that stretch us, soften us, and shape us.

A man who has been restored by Jesus begins to love differently. He listens more. He reacts less. He speaks with gentleness instead of defensiveness. He leads with humility instead of pride. He shows up with presence instead of pressure. He begins to see his wife not through the lens of his own needs, but through the lens of Christ's love.

This doesn't happen overnight. It happens in small moments — in the way he apologizes, in the way he forgives, in the way he chooses patience, in the way he chooses understanding. These are the signs of a man walking in his new identity.

A man's family — whether children, siblings, parents, or extended relatives — becomes the place where his transformation begins to ripple outward. The man who once lived guarded now becomes a safe place. The man who once lived distracted now becomes present. The man who once lived overwhelmed now becomes steady.

His children begin to feel the difference. They see the peace in his eyes. They hear the gentleness in his voice. They sense the stability in his presence. They experience the love that flows from a man who is no longer living from emptiness, but from fullness.

This is where legacy begins — not in what a man leaves behind, but in who he becomes while he is here.

Finances: Where Stewardship Replaces Stress

Finances are one of the most practical and revealing areas of a man's life. They expose fear, control, insecurity, and pressure. But when Jesus renews a man's mind, even his relationship with money begins to change.

He no longer sees finances as a measure of worth, but as a tool for stewardship.

He no longer spends from impulse, but from wisdom.

He no longer fears lack because he trusts God's provision.

He no longer carries the weight alone because he knows he is not alone.

A renewed identity brings renewed priorities. A restored heart brings restored stewardship. A man who trusts Jesus with his soul learns to trust Him with his resources.

Why This Chapter Matters

This chapter is not about giving rules. It is about showing how a restored man lives — gently, wisely, intentionally, and with a heart shaped by Christ.

I was no different.

In my earlier years, I wasn't always transparent about finances. I carried the pressure quietly. I made decisions without fully communicating. I tried to fix things on my own. I tried to be the provider without admitting when I was overwhelmed or unsure. And like many men, I learned some lessons the hard way.

But here is the grace in it: God used even my financial mistakes to teach me, shape me, and humble me. He didn't condemn me. He didn't abandon me. He didn't define me by what I mishandled. Instead, He walked with me through it. He taught me wisdom. He taught me stewardship. He taught me transparency. And He taught me that provision is not something I produce — it is something He supplies. For that, I am deeply grateful.

A renewed man doesn't pretend he has always gotten it right. He acknowledges where he fell short, and he celebrates the God who lifted him up. He learns to talk openly with his spouse about money. He learns to plan with wisdom instead of reacting with fear. He learns to trust God with what he has and with what he hopes to have. He learns that finances are not a measure of his worth — they are an opportunity to walk in stewardship, humility, and unity.

This kind of honesty is healing.

This kind of transparency is freeing.

This kind of growth is evidence of transformation.

And when a man brings this renewed posture into his marriage and family, everything changes. The home becomes lighter. The conversations become safer. The decisions become wiser. The pressure becomes shared instead of carried alone. And the man becomes a steward, not a struggler — not because he is perfect, but because he is learning.

As a restored man steps into his home, he discovers that leadership is not about control, dominance, or having all the answers. It is about presence. It is about steadiness. It is about bringing the peace Jesus has placed inside him into the rooms where his family lives, breathes, and grows. A restored man leads differently because he is different.

He begins to understand that leadership is not loud — it is consistent. It is not forceful — it is faithful. It is not about being perfect — it is about being present. His family doesn't need a flawless man; they need a man who is learning to walk with Jesus in real time.

This kind of leadership shows up in small, sacred ways.

He listens more deeply.

He apologizes more quickly.

He forgives more freely.

He speaks more gently.

He prays more honestly.

He shows up more intentionally.

These are not dramatic gestures. They are the quiet evidence of a man whose heart has been softened and strengthened by the presence of Christ.

A man who once led from pressure now leads from peace.

A man who once led from insecurity now leads from identity.

A man who once led from fear now leads from trust.

And his family feels the difference.

His wife feels safer, not because he is perfect, but because he is present. She sees the humility in him. She sees the growth. She sees the way he is learning to love her with patience, tenderness, and emotional honesty. She sees the way he is becoming a partner, not just a provider — a man who carries the home with her, not above her.

His children feel steadier, not because he never makes mistakes, but because he owns them. They see a man who is learning to be gentle. They see a man who is learning to be patient. They see a man who is learning to be consistent. They see a man who is learning to love them with the same grace Jesus has shown him.

This is leadership in its truest form — not the leadership of authority, but the leadership of example.

And even in finances, where he once struggled with transparency or carried the weight alone, he now leads with openness and humility. He invites unity instead of secrecy. He seeks wisdom instead of reacting from fear. He trusts God's provision instead of trying to control outcomes. His leadership becomes a reflection of the transformation happening inside him.

For the new believer, this is encouraging. It shows that leadership is not about knowing everything — it's about walking with Jesus and letting that walk shape the way you love your family. For the seasoned believer, it is a reminder that leadership is not a title — it is a posture.

A restored man leads his home not by being the strongest voice in the room, but by being the most surrendered heart in the room.

A restored man doesn't just lead his home — he shapes it. And he shapes it through the quiet, consistent rhythms that reflect who he is becoming in Christ.

For many men, the home used to be the place where stress showed up the strongest. The weight of work, finances, expectations, and unspoken fears often spilled into the living room, the kitchen, and the bedroom. But when Jesus begins to transform a man, the pressure that once leaked out of him becomes peace that flows from him.

He doesn't bring chaos into the home anymore.

He brings calm.

He brings steadiness.

He brings presence.

This doesn't mean he never feels pressure — it means he no longer lets pressure define the atmosphere. He has learned to take his burdens to Jesus before they become burdens to his family. He has learned to breathe, to pause, to pray, to reset. And his home becomes a place where peace is not the exception — it becomes the norm.

A Home Where Emotional Safety Becomes a Priority

A transformed man understands that emotional safety is not weakness — it is strength. It is the foundation of trust, connection, and intimacy. It is what allows his wife to open her heart without fear. It is what allows his children to come to him without hesitation.

He creates emotional safety by:

- listening without dismissing
- correcting without crushing
- guiding without controlling
- apologizing without excuses
- loving without conditions

His presence becomes a refuge. His voice becomes reassurance. His consistency becomes comfort. His humility becomes healing.

This is the fruit of a renewed mind — a man who no longer leads from ego, but from empathy.

A restored man doesn't try to be the "spiritual giant" of the home. He simply walks with Jesus in a way that is visible, honest, and natural. His family sees him pray. They see him read. They see him worship. They see him surrender. They see him grow. And because they see it, they feel invited into it.

He doesn't preach at his family — he lives before them.

He doesn't pressure them — he guides them.

He doesn't demand spiritual maturity — he models it.

This is how spiritual rhythm is formed in a home: not through rules, but through relationship. Not through force, but through example. Not through perfection, but through authenticity.

A man who has received grace becomes a man who gives grace. He doesn't hold grudges. He doesn't weaponize mistakes. He doesn't make his home a courtroom. He makes it a place where grace is practiced daily — in conversations, in corrections, in decisions, in disagreements.

His family learns that they don't have to be perfect to be loved.

They learn that mistakes are moments for growth, not shame.

They learn that forgiveness is the rhythm of the home, not the exception.

This is the culture of a transformed man — a culture shaped by the grace he has received from Jesus.

A man who has been restored begins to see his life differently. He no longer views his marriage as something to keep, but as a covenant to nurture. He no longer sees his family as a duty, but as a gift. He no longer sees his finances as a source of pressure, but as a tool for stewardship. Everything shifts because he has shifted. The renewed mind changes the way he approaches the future, and the restored heart changes the way he invests in the people around him.

As he continues to walk in this new identity, he begins to understand that legacy is not built in grand gestures—it is built in daily choices. It is built in the way he speaks to his wife when he is tired. It is built in the way he listens to his children when they need him. It is built in the way he handles money with integrity and openness. It is built in the way he shows up, day after day, as a man who is being shaped by Jesus.

For the new believer, this is a hopeful realization. He doesn't need a perfect past to build a meaningful future. He simply needs a surrendered heart and a willingness to grow. For the seasoned believer, it is a reminder that legacy is not something we leave behind when we die—it is something we live out while we are here. It is the imprint of Christ's work in us, expressed through the way we love, lead, and steward what God has entrusted to us.

• • •

REFLECT

1. In which area of your home life — marriage, parenting, or finances — have you been showing up physically but checking out emotionally?
2. What is one conversation you have been avoiding with your spouse or children that your silence has already begun to cost them?

3. If the people in your home were asked to describe the atmosphere you bring through the door each day, what would they say?

CHAPTER 20

My Children, My Joy

There are few blessings in a man's life that shape him as deeply, as tenderly, and as permanently as his children. Long before I understood the fullness of who I was in Christ, long before I learned how to walk in healing and identity, God had already placed four extraordinary gifts in my life: my twin sons, Anthony and Jared; my daughter Valencia; and my daughter Brittany, who now rests in heaven. Each of them has marked my heart in a way that time cannot erase and eternity cannot diminish.

A father's love is not something that fades. It grows. It deepens. It matures. It stretches. It survives storms, mistakes, distance, and even death. My love for each of my children is everlasting—not because I am perfect, but because God placed them in my life as part of His purpose for me. They have been my joy, my motivation, my teachers, and my reminders of God's goodness even in seasons when I didn't always see it clearly.

When I look at Anthony and Jared, my twin sons, I see strength, resilience, and the evidence of God's hand guiding them into manhood.

Watching them grow into responsible, loving husbands has been one of the greatest honors of my life. Raising two boys at the same time forced me to grow in patience, discipline, and intentionality. They showed me that leadership in the home is not about being the loudest voice, but about being the most consistent presence. As they grew into men, I watched them develop their own identities—different in personality, yet united in character. Their journey into manhood taught me that a father's role is not to mold his sons into his own image, but to guide them toward the image God placed within them. They are men of character, men of integrity, and men who carry themselves with a quiet confidence that makes a father proud. Their lives remind me that legacy is not built in perfection—it is built in presence, in love, and in the seeds planted over time.

When I look at my daughter Valencia, I see grace, beauty, and a spirit that reflects both courage and compassion. She has a way of carrying herself that reminds me of the strength God places in His daughters. She has weathered life with dignity, and her presence in my life has been a constant reminder of God's tenderness. She is a joy to me, not just because she is my daughter, but because of the woman she has become. Through her, I learned that daughters need a father who sees them, values them, and speaks life into them. Her strength, her grace, and her resilience have inspired me more than she knows. She carries a quiet power that reflects both her mother's influence and God's hand on her life.

And then there is my daughter Brittany—my baby girl who now lives in the presence of the Lord. Losing her was a pain deeper than words, a wound that reshaped my soul. But even in her absence, she is still one of my greatest joys. But her life—her smile, her spirit, her laughter—left an imprint that time cannot erase. She taught me to cherish moments, to slow down, to love deeply, and to hold my children close. Even in her passing, she continues to shape me. She reminds me that love is eternal, that heaven is real, and that the bond between a father and his child does not end at the grave. Her memory is alive in me. Her laughter still echoes in my heart. Her life still teaches me. And her place in my story is eternal. I carry her with me—not in sorrow, but in love. She is part of my joy because she is part of me, and nothing—not even death—can separate a father from the love he has for his child.

As I reflect on each of my children, I realize that they have been some of God's greatest tools in shaping me. They have taught me patience, humility, sacrifice, and unconditional love. They have shown me my strengths and exposed my weaknesses. They have given me reasons to grow, reasons to heal, and reasons to keep becoming the man God intended me to be.

This chapter is not about my success as a father—it is about the grace of God expressed through the lives of my children. They are my joy. They are my legacy. They are the evidence that even in my imperfect journey, God has been faithful.

There are seasons in a man's life when he thinks he is shaping his children, only to look back and realize that his children were shaping him just as deeply. Each of my children—Anthony, Jared, Valencia, and Brittany—has marked my life in a way that cannot be measured. They have stretched me, softened me, challenged me, and taught me lessons I could not have learned any other way. When I think about the man I am today, I see their fingerprints all over my growth. They were not just part of my story; they helped write it.

Together, my children taught me how to love in ways I didn't know I was capable of. They taught me humility when I failed, grace when I stumbled, and perseverance when life felt heavy. They taught me that fatherhood is not about perfection—it is about presence. It is about showing up, learning, growing, and loving with everything you have. They helped me become a better man, a better father, and a better follower of Christ.

A father's love matures over time, shaped by the seasons he walks through and the lessons life insists on teaching him. When I look back over the years, I can see how each season—whether filled with laughter, challenge, or heartbreak—deepened my understanding of what it means to love my children. That love did not stay the same; it grew as I grew. It became wiser, steadier, and more rooted in grace.

In the early years, my love was expressed through protection and provision. I wanted to shield my children from harm and give them the best foundation I could. As they grew older, that love shifted into guidance and encouragement. I learned that fatherhood is not about controlling outcomes, but about walking beside them as they discover who they are. Watching them step into adulthood taught me to release them into God's hands, trusting that He would finish the work He began in them.

As life unfolded, my love matured even further. I learned to appreciate their individuality, their strengths, and the unique paths God carved out for them. I learned to listen more deeply, to speak more thoughtfully, and to celebrate the people they were becoming. I discovered that a father's love is not measured by how much he can do for his children, but by how present he is in their lives—how willing he is to grow, to apologize, to forgive, and to keep showing up.

And then came the season of loss, the season that reshaped my heart in ways I never expected. Losing a child is a pain that has no language. It is a wound that time does not erase. Yet even in that grief, love did not diminish—it expanded. It became more tender, more sacred, more aware of the fragility and beauty of life. It taught me to cherish every moment, to hold my children close, and to trust God with the pieces of my heart that now live in heaven. Love became something eternal, something that stretches beyond this world and into the presence of God.

Through all these seasons, I discovered that fatherhood is not a role—it is a calling. It is a journey of becoming, of learning, of surrendering, and of loving with a heart that is continually being shaped by God. My children have been my joy not because life has been perfect, but because they have been part of every chapter of my growth. They have taught me more about love, grace, and resilience than I could have ever learned on my own.

A father's love is shaped over time—through seasons of joy, seasons of challenge, and seasons that leave a permanent mark on the soul. As I look back over my life, I can see how each season with my children deepened me. They refined my patience, expanded my compassion, and taught me a quality of love I could never have discovered on my own.

• • •

REFLECT

1. When was the last time you allowed yourself to cry? What happened?
2. What would it mean to see tears not as weakness but as the language of a waking heart?
3. What are you holding right now that you need to release to God in this moment?

CHAPTER 21

Sometimes Men Cry

I have cried. I want to say that plainly before anything else in this chapter, because I am asking you to go somewhere in these pages that men are not usually asked to go, and I will not ask you to go there without going first.

I cried over my daughter Brittany. In private, in the dark, in the kind of silence that only grief produces — the silence where the world keeps moving and you cannot understand how, because something fundamental has stopped. I have sat with that loss in moments where I had no words for God and no performance left in me, and the only thing that came out was tears. And I let them come. And God was there. Not with answers. Not with explanation. Just there — which was, in those moments, everything.

I have cried over my failures. Over seasons when I was not the husband or the father, I should have been, where the cost of my silence and my pride showed up in the faces of people I loved, and I had to sit with what that meant. That kind of crying is different from grief. It is heavier in some ways, because it comes with the weight of knowing you could have done differently. But it is also the crying that breaks something loose in a man — the crying that finally lets you stop defending yourself and start becoming something better.

I have cried over things I could not name. The kind of exhaustion that has no specific cause but settles into your bones after years of carrying what you were never designed to carry alone. Men know that crying. It is the one that surprises you — in a quiet moment, in the car, in the shower, in the middle of a worship song that hits somewhere you did not know was still tender. You are not even sure what started it. You just know something in you needed to release.

I am telling you this because I need you to hear it from a man.

Not as a concept. Not as permission granted from a safe theological distance. From a man who has been exactly where you are, who was raised the same way you were raised, who heard the same messages you heard — and who found out the hard way that holding all of it in was not strength. It was just postponing the inevitable.

THE TRUTH ABOUT YOUR TEARS

Your tears are not a sign that you have failed.

They are a sign that you have been strong for too long. They are the release valve of a soul that has carried more than it was designed to hold alone. They are evidence that your heart is still alive — still tender, still reachable, still capable of being moved. And a heart that can be moved is a heart that can be healed.

When a man cries, heaven does not turn away.

Heaven draws near.

When your life cracks open, that's the moment God moves toward you. Not after you've cleaned yourself up — right then, in the middle of what feels like destruction. There's no audition for His attention, no version of you He's waiting to see first. Come tired. Come angry. Come with the tears you've been swallowing for years. The brokenhearted aren't a problem He tolerates; they're the ones He chases. And brother, if your heart is in pieces, He already knows your name and He's already on His way.

Your tears do not make you less of a man.

They make you honest.

They make you human.

And sometimes — not always, but sometimes — they make you free in a way that nothing else could.

Some men cry because the burden has been heavy for years and the body finally refuses to carry what the mind insists on suppressing. Some cry because they are exhausted from being the strong one, the steady one, the one everyone else leans on, and there is simply nothing left to perform with. Some cry because God is doing something in them — softening what life hardened, opening what pain closed, reaching the places that every other approach could not get to.

And some men cry because healing has finally begun. Because something in them has decided that the cost of hiding is too high. Because they have read words in a book or heard a song or sat in a quiet room long enough to finally feel the weight of what they have been carrying — and they have decided, maybe for the first time, to put it down.

Whatever brings the tears, they are not wasted.

Not one of them.

THIS IS WHAT THE WHOLE BOOK HAS BEEN ABOUT

We started at the mask. The one you put on before you even understood you were putting it on. The one that got built out of playgrounds and living rooms and the quiet lesson that a man's job is to appear unaffected by things that affect him deeply.

We walked through the cost of silence, the weight of expectations that nobody actually placed on you but that you have been trying to meet anyway. We talked about what it takes to feel again, to trust again, to be honest enough with yourself and with God to bring your actual life to Him instead of the managed version.

We talked about wholeness — not as a destination you arrive at but as a way of living, a daily decision to show up as the same man in private that you are in public.

And now we are here. At the end of the road and the beginning of a new one.

I do not know exactly where you are as you read these words. I do not know what you have been carrying or how long you have been carrying it. I do not know what the mask has cost you, or who is waiting on the other side of your honesty, or what God has been trying to reach in you that the performance has been blocking.

But I know this:

You picked up this book for a reason.

Something in you was ready. Maybe not for everything — maybe just for one honest conversation with yourself, one prayer that doesn't have its edges smoothed off, one moment where you stop pretending that you are fine when you are not. That is enough. That is where it starts.

MEN, GIVE YOURSELVES A BREAK.

Not because you are weak.

Because you are worthy of healing.

Not because you have failed.

Because God has not finished.

Not because you deserve pity.

Because you deserve peace — real peace, the kind that does not depend on everything going right, the kind that holds even when life is hard and the answers don't come and the grief is still present, and the regret is still real. The peace that Philippians 4:7 describes as surpassing understanding. The peace that only comes to a man who has finally stopped trying to manufacture it on his own and has opened his hands to receive it.

You are not the sum of your mistakes.

You are not the weight of your regrets.

You are not the worst thing you have ever done or the best thing you have ever managed to appear.

You are a man in process. A man becoming. A man that God looked at before you were born and said — that one. I have plans for that one. And nothing you have done since then, nothing you have hidden or failed or broken or lost, has changed that declaration.

So, if the tears come — let them come.

If the grief rises — let it rise.

If the memories surface — let them surface.

Not to undo you.

To free you.

Because that is what tears do in the hands of God. They do not end the story. They water the ground where the next chapter grows.

I am grateful — more than I know how to say — that God did not give up on me in my silent seasons. That He waited through my performance and my pride and my insistence on appearing capable until I was finally tired enough to stop. That He met me, every single time, not with judgment but with the quiet steadiness of a Father who had never left.

He will meet you there too.

He already is.

Sometimes men cry.

And in those tears, God begins the work of making us whole.

• • •

REFLECT

1. When was the last time you cried — or wanted to but held it back? What were you afraid would happen if you didn't?
2. What is one burden you have been carrying alone that you are ready, right now, to lay down?
3. What would you say to God if you knew He was sitting across from you, unhurried, with nothing but time and love — and no judgment?

Final Thoughts

The Journey a Man Takes with Himself and with God

There comes a moment in every man's life when he looks back over the road he has traveled and realizes that the journey was never just about the events, the mistakes, the victories, or the losses. It was about who he became along the way. It was about the man God was shaping beneath the surface, even when he didn't recognize the process. He carries something now he didn't have before—the quiet awareness that transformation is not a single moment, but a lifetime of becoming.

A man does not arrive at healing all at once. He grows into it. He steps into it. He learns to trust it. He learns to believe that God's grace is big enough to cover his past and strong enough to carry his future. He learns that the things he once thought would break him were actually the very things God used to build him. He learns that the wounds he carried were not signs of weakness, but invitations to deeper surrender. And he learns that the love of God is not something he earns—it is something he receives.

As he reflects on his life, he begins to see the threads of God's faithfulness woven through every season. He sees the moments when he should have fallen apart but didn't. He sees the times when he felt alone but was carried. He sees the doors that closed for his protection and the ones that opened for his growth. He sees the people God placed in his life to guide him, challenge him, love him, and remind him of who he truly is. And he sees the man he has become—not perfect, but transformed; not flawless, but faithful; not finished, but firmly in the hands of God.

These thoughts are not about tying everything together neatly. Life rarely works that way. Instead, it is about acknowledging the beauty of the journey—the highs, the lows, the lessons, the breakthroughs, and the quiet moments when God whispered truth into a weary heart. It is about recognizing that every chapter of a man's life has purpose, even the ones he wishes he could rewrite. It is about embracing the truth that God wastes nothing—not the pain, not the joy, not the mistakes, not the victories.

A man who has walked through healing learns to see himself differently. He no longer defines himself by what he lost, but by what God restored. He no longer sees himself through the lens of shame, but through the lens of grace. He no longer carries the weight of who he used to be, because he has learned to walk in the freedom of who he is becoming. And he no longer fears the future because he knows the One who holds it.

Walking with God is not something a man graduates from—it is something he grows into. The transformation he has experienced, the healing he has embraced, and the identity he has learned to walk in are not destinations; they are foundations. They are the beginning of a new way of living, a new way of seeing himself, and a new way of trusting God with every step ahead.

A man who has walked through brokenness and found restoration learns to see God differently. He no longer sees God as distant or demanding, but as present and patient. He recognizes that God was with him in the moments he didn't understand, in the seasons he didn't think he would survive, and in the chapters he thought were too painful to redeem. He begins to understand that God's faithfulness was not just something he read about—it was something he lived through.

As he moves forward, he carries with him a deeper awareness of God's presence. He learns to invite God into the ordinary moments, not just the crises. He learns to talk to God with honesty, not performance. He learns to listen for God's voice in the quiet places, not just the dramatic ones. And he learns that walking with God is not about perfection—it is about relationship. It is about trust. It is about surrender. It is about choosing, day by day, to let God lead.

This new way of walking shapes everything. It shapes the way he loves. It shapes the way he forgives. It shapes the way he handles pressure, disappointment, and uncertainty. It shapes the way he sees his purpose and the way he steps into his future. He no longer walks as a man defined by his past, but as a man guided by God's hand. He no longer carries the weight of who he used to be, because he has learned to rest in who God is making him.

And as he continues this journey, he discovers that God is not finished with him. There are still places to grow, still lessons to learn, still blessings to receive, still people to love, still purpose to fulfill. The man he is becoming is not the final version—he is the ongoing work of a faithful God. Every new season becomes an opportunity to trust God more deeply, to love more freely, and to walk more confidently in the identity he has been given.

There comes a time in a man's life when he realizes that everything he has walked through—every joy, every wound, every lesson, every moment of grace—has been shaping him for a purpose far greater than he once understood. Purpose is not something a man stumbles into; it is something he grows into. It is revealed through the journey, refined through the struggles, and strengthened through the healing. Each life lesson turns toward that deeper truth: that a man who has been transformed is now equipped to live with intention, clarity, and a sense of calling that flows from the heart of God.

As he steps into this new season, he begins to understand that calling is not limited to a title, a position, or a platform. Calling is the expression of who he is becoming in Christ. It is the way he shows up in the world. It is the way he carries the lessons he has learned. It is the way he reflects God's heart in the spaces he occupies. Whether he is speaking to a crowd, encouraging a friend, guiding his family, or simply living with integrity, he is walking in his calling. His life becomes a message—one written not with perfection, but with authenticity and grace.

Legacy, too, takes on a new meaning. It is no longer about what he accumulates or accomplishes, but about what he deposits into the lives of others. Legacy is the imprint of his character, the echo of his love, the fruit of his growth, and the testimony of God's faithfulness in his life. It is the way his children remember him, the way his friends respect him, the way his community feels his presence, and the way his story continues long after he is gone. A man who has walked with God leaves behind more than memories—he leaves behind seeds that continue to grow.

As he reflects on his journey, he realizes that nothing was wasted. The mistakes taught him humility. The losses taught him compassion. The victories taught him gratitude. The healing taught him surrender. And the transformation taught him that God's purpose is always bigger than the pain that preceded it. He steps into the rest of his life with a quiet confidence—not in himself, but in the God who has carried him this far and will carry him the rest of the way.

As a man grows in his identity, he begins to understand that God is not asking him to be perfect—He is asking him to be present. Present with Him. Present with himself. Present with the people he loves. God invites him into a life where honesty replaces hiding, where surrender replaces striving, and where trust replaces fear. This is the life a healed man learns to embrace: a life where he no longer carries everything alone, because he knows he was never meant to.

Walking with God becomes less about performance and more about connection. It becomes less about trying to impress God and more about learning to rest in Him. It becomes less about proving something and more about receiving what God freely gives. A man who walks with God learns to bring Him into the ordinary moments—the quiet mornings, the long drives, the difficult conversations, the decisions that weigh on his heart. He learns that God is not only present in the breakthroughs; He is present in the small, steady steps that make up a man's life.

This kind of walk shapes a man's character. It softens what life hardened. It strengthens what fear weakened. It clarifies what confusion clouded. It steadies what once felt unstable. And it teaches him that the same God who healed him is the God who will guide him. He begins to trust that God's voice is not distant or complicated—it is gentle, consistent, and always leading him toward life.

Thank you for sharing this healing journey with me.

A Prayer for the Man Who's Becoming Whole

Father. Thank You for every man who has walked through these pages with an open heart. Thank You for meeting him in the places he has hidden, the places he has feared, and the places he has carried alone for far too long. Thank You for reminding him that he is not forgotten, not forsaken, and not beyond Your reach.

Lord, teach him to breathe again. Teach him to rest in Your love. Teach him to trust that he does not have to be perfect to be held by You.

Where he has carried shame, replace it with grace.

Where he has carried regret, replace it with redemption.

Where he has carried silence, give him a new voice.

Where he has carried tears, remind him that You collect everyone.

Father, restore the places that life has broken. Heal the wounds he never had words for. Lift the burdens he was never meant to carry alone. Strengthen the parts of him that grew weary from pretending to be strong.

Let him know—deep in his soul—that he is loved.

Not for what he produces.

Not for what he hides.

Not for how well he performs.

But simply because he is Your son.

Teach him to forgive himself the way You have forgiven him.

Teach him to walk in freedom, not fear.

Teach him to lead with tenderness, courage, and truth.

Teach him to love without armor and to stand without shame.

Lord, remind him that his story is not over.

That his failures are not final.

That his tears are not signs of weakness, but signs of life.

And that every step he takes toward healing is a step toward You.

Cover him with Your peace.

Surround him with Your presence.

Guide him with Your wisdom.

And shape him into the man You designed him to be—whole, steady, restored, and unafraid to feel.

Thank You for the journey You have begun in him.

Thank You that You will finish what You started.

And thank You that even when he stumbles, Your grace is still enough.

In Jesus' name,

Amen.

About the Author

David Proctor is an associate minister, author, and mentor whose life's work centers on guiding men toward emotional honesty, spiritual healing, and authentic transformation. Known for his gentle, pastoral voice and his ability to speak truth with compassion, David has spent years walking with men through the hidden battles of the heart—helping them rediscover their identity, reclaim their purpose, and embrace the grace of God without shame.

Born and raised in a family rooted in faith, David carries forward the legacy of his parents, Wardell and Mary Proctor, whose love and example shaped his early understanding of strength, humility, and perseverance. His journey has been marked by seasons of joy, loss, growth, and deep reflection—experiences that have shaped his ministry and given him a unique ability to speak to the hearts of men with authenticity and authority.

David's life is anchored by his wife, Shannon, whose love, and partnership have strengthened him through every chapter of his story. He is the proud father of Anthony, Jared, Valencia, and Brittany—each of whom has shaped him in profound ways. The loss of his daughter Brittany became a defining moment in his spiritual journey, deepening his compassion and expanding his understanding of God's healing presence.

Through his writing, David invites men to step out of silence, release the weight they've carried, and discover the freedom found in vulnerability and faith. His message is simple yet powerful: men are allowed to be human, to feel deeply, to heal fully, and to walk boldly in the identity God has given them.

www.ingramcontent.com/pod-product-compliance
Lightning Source LLC
LaVergne TN
LVHW010703110826
845149LV00014B/3214

9798996255115